BEST OF SCOTLAND

For
Miss Margaret Hogg,
who taught us we were Scottish;
taught me to see

BEST OF SCOTLAND

JOHN MACLEOD

BIRLINN

First published in 2019 by
Birlinn Limited West Newington House
10 Newington Road Edinburgh EH9 1QS www.birlinn.co.uk

ISBN 9781780272016

British Library Cataloguing-in-Publication Data A catalogue record for this book is
available from the British Library

Typeset in Gill Sans
Design: seagulls.net
Printed and bound in China

INTRODUCTION

The best thing about a book like this is how you can enthuse about so many wonderfully Scottish things – Robert Burns, the soaring eagle, the high girders of the Forth Bridge, lochs and castles and tweed and paddle-steamers, and even both our national drinks.

The most gutting is how much you have to leave out. There was, sadly, no room in the end for John Buchan and Muriel Spark, midgies and Taggart, Sir Walter Scott, Edinburgh's One O'Clock Gun and mouth-watering tablet. And some themes, of course, are compulsory. Anyone writing a book like this who left out tartan, haggis and bagpipes would probably be arrested.

Scotland is a land of heroes and builders, the highest mountains in Britain and the deepest inland water in Europe – renowned for our inventors, our songs and our castles, which is just as well, considering our football.

I thank Hugh Andrew for the idea, Andrew Simmons for his sustained interest and support – and remind myself that behind every successful author is an astonished editor.

John MacLeod
Marybank, Isle of Lewis

CONTENTS

01

CALLANISH STONES

Massed and eerie atop a ridge on the Isle of Lewis in the Outer Hebrides, the Standing Stones of Callanish are the most important remains of prehistoric Scotland.

Reflecting a lost, ancient but sophisticated culture – a society evidently capable of agriculture, engineering, mathematics and astronomy – there is something faintly unnerving about these megaliths. At dusk, or in mist, they seem almost human. Indeed, the old Gaelic name for them in the district was *fir bhrèige*, meaning 'false men'.

These stones were old before a word of Gaelic was spoken on the island. And, though in final form the layout is very similar to a Celtic cross, they had been standing for 2,000 years before the birth of Christ.

They are appreciated at their best on a fine day in winter, when the sun hangs over the island hills and there aren't busloads of people clucking about. Quickly you sense that the siting of these great slabs of Lewisian gneiss is no accident. This is a commanding spot, with fine views and long, long sightlines.

You also grasp that their builders cannot have been the cavemen of a child's imagination, forever dragging bits of mammoth home and saying, 'Ug'.

To haul these stones a considerable distance – the quarry obviously used is a mile away – called for society, leadership and organisation. That these stones have stood for so long testifies to the skill of their erection (they are rooted firmly in sockets of wedged stone and boulder-clay; only a fifth of each megalith is below ground level). And, if you think about it, you eventually figure that they can only have been transported here on rollers – which means logs, which means that this bare landscape of moor and water must, way back then, have been heavily wooded.

In fact, we know from pollen samples that the climate and flora of Lewis were, thousands of years ago, very different to today – much more akin, say experts, to that of southern France. We also know, simply by looking around the area, that for some reason this corner of Lewis was an important centre, for there are several other stone circles in and around Callanish and more to be found in the wider district of western Lewis.

This site – Callanish I – is the biggest, most complex and important, with its radiating wings, southern avenue and central circle, a big behemoth of a stone in the middle and the ruined chambered cairn.

It wasn't all put up at once, as archaeologists have recently established. Crops were grown here and a curved ditch was dug before any stone was lofted upright. Later there was a wooden palisade round the site. Only after that was a bare circle of standing stones erected – likely hauled here by sled.

The wings and avenue were added subsequently, and the chambered cairn – evidently a tomb – was last of all. In the first millennium BC the climate changed, the weather grew much cooler and damper, peat began steadily to rise on Lewis and by 500 BC the Callanish Stones seem to have been closed for business. The society that had erected and cherished them simply ceased to exist.

The essential points to grasp are that the complex was erected and embellished during the best part of 2,000 years – suggesting changing

emphases, rituals and priorities. And if you ask, 'What were the Callanish Stones for?', there is no one-word answer.

In fact, this site served many purposes – and most of them, likely, at the same time. This was a community centre, a university, a theatre of public ceremony, a place of worship, a place – perhaps – of court proceedings and even executions … But we can be pretty certain that all these revolved around the prime function of observatory.

For this is a brilliant place to watch the skies. This far north the sun by day and the moon by night can be followed along a very long arc. And the peaks, troughs and summits of all those island hills allowed the movements of heavenly bodies, through months and over years, to be plotted precisely. Those who ran Callanish would, in time, have compiled a most accurate almanac. And their ability to predict tides, eclipses and so on – to mark the months of the year and the hours of the day – would have given them considerable status and power.

It's important not to exaggerate the claims of some recent boffins. A lot of alleged alignments at Callanish have been debunked and the few undoubted ones may simply have been chance. But there is hard evidence for the observatory thesis.

For one, when viewed in exact line from the crag overlooking the stones from the east, the pillars of the south row run true from south to north. It is especially impressive because four millennia ago the star we now call Polaris was not near the North Celestial Pole; our planet's axis of rotation has since moved in relation to the night sky.

For another, it has been demonstrated – over decades of earnest, private study by Margaret Curtis – that the stones are perfectly designed to follow every movement of the moon through the so-called 'lunar year' – the span of 18.61 years that it takes the Queen of the Night to complete her cycle of every possible variation in moonrise and moonset.

And one event in this dance, the Major Lunar Standstill, when she reaches the very southern extreme of her course, is viewed to spectacular effect from the avenue at Callanish, leaving little doubt – for Mrs Curtis's thesis has now been tested twice, at the standstills of 1987 and 2006 – that the final layout was for this very purpose.

Sadly, though hundreds of gentle, faintly eccentric people visit Lewis late every June to make the most, in their earnest way, of the longest day of the year, there is not a shred of evidence that the stones have anything at all to do with the Midsummer Solstice.

DID YOU KNOW?

The Callanish Stones, believed to have been built shortly after 3000 BC, consist of a central circle of 13 stones, from which four alignments extend to form a general cross shape.

Within the central circle is a burial chamber. Excavations have shown that this was added a few generations after the stones were erected, but it is a mystery as to who instructed this construction, and why.

There are several smaller stone circles near Callanish, such as Cnoc Ceann a'Gharraidh, a circle of eight stones, and Cnoc Fillibhir Bheag, a double circle with eight stones in the outer ring and four in the inner ring.

It is thought that the Callanish Stones may have been used throughout the ages to observe the movements of the moon.

02

WHISKY

An uisge-beatha, the water of life, the amber nectar – and our national drink, only ever referred to as whisky, this side of the Border, though 'Scotch' in England and America.

And, sadly, no one knows who invented it – though we know, from a surviving docket accompanying a load of malt to 'Friar John Cor, by order of the king, to make aquavitae' – that it's been around since at least 1494.

It was not till the nineteenth century, though, that it began to be hedged about in law and when distilling your own whisky became illegal. 'Scotch Whisky' can only be made in Scotland, it can only be made with water and malted barley (to which only wholegrains of other cereals can be added), and it must be matured (in 154-gallon wooden casks) in an excise warehouse, in Scotland, for at least three years.

There are two kinds – malt whisky and blended whisky – and until the 1970s bottled malt whisky was actually very difficult for ordinary people to buy. A malt whisky is made at a specific local distillery whose names read as if they should be accompanied by marching pipers – Glenfiddich, Glenlivet, Glenmorangie, Talisaker, Laphroaig and dozens more – and each 'single malt' has its own unique character. Sample a dram of Highland Park, from Orkney, and you get a big hit of peat; the celebrated malts from Islay, most southerly and most fertile of all the Hebrides, have notes of iodine, seaweed and even a hint of salt.

Blended whisky is made with grain-alcohol (usually maize) distilled much less romantically, with up to 40% of various malts added to lend interest – perhaps up to 20 different malts. And blends are by no means to be despised; it takes great skill to make a product consistent in taste and bouquet. The late Princess Margaret went nowhere without her Famous Grouse, and some of our best blends are actually seldom seen in Scotland – Dewar's and J&B are among the respected whiskies largely exported.

Whisky barrels lined up on the shores of the Isle of Islay, Inner Hebrides.

Malt whisky begins with whole grains of barley soaked in water for between 50 and 60 hours and then transferred to a concrete floor, where it is spread at a depth of about three feet. The barley soon begins to sprout, which generates heat, and the attentive malt-men keep turning and spreading the grain with a special wooden shovel called a 'skip'. This keeps each seed germinating at the same rate, and also prevents their rootlets from being entangled.

It takes about twelve days before the rootlets wither; the grain becomes chalky and you then have malt. (Some distilleries now turn the malt mechanically and a few, these days, no longer do their own malting at all but buy malt ready-made.) Now it is spread on a wire-mesh floor in a kiln, where it is dried over a fire – traditionally peat – to stop the germination. Peat and the other pyrogens within it (like ancient seaweed) add interesting and exquisite notes to the dram that will finally splash in your glass.

Germination produces an enzyme, diastase, which then converts the starch in the barley to a soluble sugar, $C_{12}H_{22}O_{11}$ – maltose. The malt is now ground and washed four times with hot water in a huge 'mash tun' to extract all the maltose in solution. What's left over, the 'draff', is a prized food for cattle. Now we have a liquid called 'wort,' which is cooled to about 80°F and put into a vast wooden 'wash-back' – 5,000 gallons or more in capacity – with a special sort of yeast. The yeast has two enzymes, maltase – which turns the maltose to glucose – and zymase, which then turns that glucose to alcohol.

At last we have 'wash', which can be transferred to the gleaming, curvy copper pot-still. What emerges are the 'low wines'. These are then run into the spirit-still and distilled a second time and – to make a long story boring – you end up with a clear, colourless liquid of 15° to 20° 'over proof'. You dilute

Many varieties of whisky on display in Tomintoul, the highest village in the Highlands.

this with spring water to 11° over proof, and then pour it into an oak cask and wait at least three years. These casks are a tale in themselves. Depending where you are, they may be newly made on site by your own cooper or second-hand ones that have previously held sherry or bourbon – and all must be internally 'toasted'. This is a dramatic process – columns of swirling flame – and brings other elements of flavour (and colour) to the party.

Many believe whisky should in fact be matured for at least five years, with eight to twelve the optimal – by fifteen, the whisky has gone off. Inevitably, some evaporates over the years, and thus Scots joke of the 'angels' share'.

Scotch whisky is classified by six regions – Highland, Speyside, Lowland, Campbeltown, Islay and Islands – and whiskies made in each of these areas have broadly similar characteristics. In recent years a number of entrepreneurs have opened new distilleries in, especially, the Hebrides, on islands such as Lewis, Harris and Raasay, where whisky has not lawfully been made in two centuries.

Please don't defile your glass of whisky with, say, lemonade, or plunge it into a mass of ice. A splash of plain water, though, will draw fully forth its particular array of flavours, as you muse that all the whisky Scotland exported in 2017 earned a cool £4.6 billion for the British economy.

03

HONOURS OF SCOTLAND

The Scottish regalia – properly known as the 'Honours of Scotland' – are the oldest crown jewels in the British Isles.

For England's were broken up and sold by Oliver Cromwell's administration after the overthrow of King Charles I, and those used today were fashioned only after the Restoration in 1660. All that survives of the originals is a twelfth-century silver-gilt anointing spoon.

The Honours managed, among other adventures, to go missing for over a century, but they still star in the Royal coats-of-arms of Scotland and the United Kingdom, and are one of many visitor attractions at

Edinburgh Castle, housed behind the toughest glass in a redoubtable strongroom.

The Crown of Scotland is fashioned of real Scottish gold, adorned with twenty-two gemstones, twenty more precious stones and lustrous pearls from freshwater mussels. The four arches are decorated with red-and-gold enamelled oak leaves – thought to be of French craftsmanship – and the gold orb where they meet is ornamented in blue enamel and with gilt stars. The cross atop is of black-and-gold enamel, with a central, rectangular amethyst.

As we see it today, it is as re-fashioned in 1540, by Edinburgh goldsmith John Mosman, at the orders of King James V, who duly wore it later that year at the crowning of his Queen, Mary of Guise-Lorraine. But the original is perhaps a good deal older, and can be seen in the 1503 'Book of Hours' portrait of his father, James IV. The Crown weighs 3lb 10 oz. (1.64 kg) and

The three crown jewels known as the 'Honours of Scotland' – the crown, the sceptre, and the Sword of State are the oldest royal regalia in Britain.

must have been very uncomfortable in the course of a long ceremony. Both James's daughter, Mary, and her own successor, James VI, were spared its weight – they acceded as infants – but Charles I enjoyed a separate Scottish coronation in 1633 (he is still our last monarch to have been born in Scotland) and his son, Charles II, was crowned King of Scots at Scone on 1 January 1650, in his tottery first reign before flight to France after defeat at Worcester.

We know exactly how old the Sceptre of Scotland is, for it was a 1494 gift to King James IV from the infamous Borgia pope, Alexander VI. It is made of silver-gilt with a polished stone (probably a cairngorm) and a pearl at the finial, and is decorated with a variety of Roman Catholic symbols – dolphins, the Virgin and Child, St James the Great and St Andrew with a saltire. The sceptre was reworked and lengthened in 1536.

The Sword of State of Scotland was also a present from a Pope – Julius II, in this instance – who gave it to James IV in 1507. It is four and a half feet long (1.4 metres), and bears the Pontiff's name, as well as images of St Peter and St Paul. The silver-gilt hilt has acorn and oak-tree motifs; and the scabbard, of wood, is clad in velvet and silver and hangs from a silk and thread-of-gold belt. The sword was badly damaged when hidden hastily (with everything else) from Cromwell's men in 1652; snapped in half for better concealment.

The Honours sat out the Commonwealth first in Dunottar Castle, south of Aberdeen, and then (when it was besieged) under the floor of Kinneff Parish Church, just north of Inverbervie. And, though readily recovered at the Restoration in 1660, they never served at a Coronation again – indeed, from 1652 to 1822, no reigning monarch even set foot in Scotland; instead, they were taken to regular diets of the Scottish Parliament as symbolic representation of the absent sovereign. With the Act of Union of 1707, this role was stripped from the Honours and they were almost casually tucked away.

More than a century later, Sir Walter Scott felt they should be unearthed; and, happily, the Prince Regent (a big fan of his novels) insisted on dinner in 1815. Sir Walter was confident he knew where the regalia were – in the long-sealed Crown Room of Edinburgh Castle – and the future George IV gladly granted permission to have this forced. On 4 February 1818, a party of burly men set to work, with Sir Walter and the Governor of the Castle as witnesses.

Mighty doors of oak and iron had to be breached, then a formidable chest was found in all the gloom. This, too, took time to open. Therein lay folded linen cloth and amidst these wrappings, dusty but intact, were the Honours of Scotland. (It is said one oaf picked up the Crown and was about to perch it on his own head when Sir Walter snapped, 'Stop!')

In short order the regalia were put on permanent, public display in the castle and have been there ever since, save for occasional ceremonial outings – and their covert burial, within the castle precincts, in 1941, lest the Germans invade. They remained out of sight until 24 June 1953, when the current Queen – newly crowned – came to Scotland's capital to be formally presented with them at St Giles Cathedral. Alas, the inexperienced young Queen arrived amidst all the gorgeously arrayed peers, clergy and officers-of-state in the most inappropriate, boring day-clothes.

To the bewildered public, fuzzy press snaps suggested Her Majesty had actually turned up in a raincoat. Her usual hideous handbag got in the way and she failed actually to don the crown of her Scots forefathers. Badly advised by her Principal

Embued with over 500 years of Scottish history, immensely precious, extremely well guarded, the Honours of Scotland are one of the prize exhibits at Edinburgh Castle.

Private Secretary, Sir Alan Lascelles, she had caused enormous offence. It is still darkly spoken of.

With the restoration of a (devolved) Scottish Parliament in 1999, the Honours have had a new role. The Crown of Scotland was brought to the official opening that July, with the Queen in attendance; to the inauguration of the permanent Holyrood home of the Parliament in September 2004, again by the Queen; and to subsequent opening ceremonies of each new Session. The Sceptre and the Sword of State are now thought too fragile to join it on these outings.

04

EILEAN DONAN

Eilean Donan is a little island – or a very large rock – in Wester Ross, positioned where three arms of seawater meet: Loch Duich, Loch Long and Loch Alsh.

And its castle, framed against dramatic mountain scenery and reached by an elegant stone bridge, is famed the world over.

Traces of ancient, vitrified stone attest to an Iron Age fort on this site. In the Christian era there was a chapel dedicated to St Donnan of Eigg, a brave Irishman of the Celtic Church who tried to evangelise the Picts.

In the early thirteenth century, during the reign of Alexander II, a large castle was first erected, enclosing much of the island – for it sat then on a critical border, between the Norse-Celtic Lordship of the Isles and

the bounds of the Earl of Ross, whose allegiance was to the King of Scots. Control of Eilean Donan greatly minimised attacks from the sea and the landing of raiders who could then penetrate deep through the glens.

The stronghold seems to have been entrusted initially to the Mathesons, then to the MacKenzies – another biddable clan who themselves garrisoned Eilean Donan with MacRaes and MacLennans. However, the MacKenzies were ambitious, clever and in close command of the West Highland seaboard, and after the Treaty of Perth in 1266 (when Magnus IV of

21

Norway finally ceded the Hebrides to King Alexander III) refused to hand back the fort to William, Earl of Ross, who was rather keen to collar the Hebrides for himself. Feuding continued for many a long year, amidst the endeavours of successive Stewart monarchs to bring the clans to heel.

It would be King James IV who finally smashed the Lordship of the Isles, late in the fifteenth century. But it left a fateful power-vacuum not, arguably, resolved until after the Battle of Culloden. These were terrible, bloody centuries for the Highlands: pitched clan battles, ceaseless feuding, forced marriages, murders, massacres and atrocities – and Kintail was a particularly intractable district and its denizens exceedingly violent people.

The MacRaes, of indefatigable loyalty to the MacKenzies – someone described them as the MacKenzies' 'shirt of mail' – are most closely associated with the castle; and further bolstered their position by cosy links with the Frasers of Lovat; you can still read a tablet inside proclaiming (in Gaelic) 'As long as there is a MacRae inside, there will never be a Fraser outside.'

It was the Jacobite movement, though, and the 1719 Rising in particular, which at last did for the old Eilean Donan, identified by its leaders as the ideal beach-head for a contingent of Spanish troops. They would be followed swiftly by a vast Spanish invasion force and a general Highland uprising.

Alas, though Eilean Donan was fast garrisoned with Spanish soldiers, the locals largely refused to revolt; the main Spanish assault never materialised and the Royal Navy – loyal, of course, to King George I – got to Eilean Donan first. After the Spaniards rebuffed a first offer of truce, the massed cannon of HMS *Worcester*, Flamborough and Enterprise then fired and fired …

By the following evening, the dazed survivors in what was left of Eilean Donan Castle surrendered with little resistance, the *Worcester*'s log smugly

recording that therein were found only 'an Irishman, a captain, a Spanish lieutenant, a serjeant, one Scotch rebel and 39 Spanish soldiers, 343 barrels of powder and 52 barrels of musquet shot'. King George's men then spent two days and twenty-seven barrels of powder in comprehensive demolition; a month later, on 10 June, what was left of the 1719 Rising was handily defeated at the Battle of Glenshiel.

And that was that for 200 years. In 1912, the splendidly named John MacRae-Gilstrap bought Eilean Donan. Born in the Punjab in 1861, and of the MacRaes of Conchra, he had a credible claim to be the Clan Chief (though there are three contenders, and the Lord Lyon King of Arms has refused ever to recognise any of them).

In 1896, under terms of his father-in-law's will – MacRae had married Isabella Gilstrap in 1889 – he bolted her name to his and took possession of a large chunk of the family maltster business and a considerable fortune.

MacRae-Gilstrap seems first to have been minded to keep Eilean Donan as so much romantic rubble but was eventually swayed by a local stonemason, Farquhar MacRae, who announced he had had a dream 'in which he saw, in the most vivid detail, exactly the way the castle originally looked'. So in 1919, MacRae-Gilstrap committed himself to reconstruction and hired an architect, George Mackie Watson.

It took twelve years, including construction of the arched stone bridge and some elements of memorial for the dead (and especially the MacRae dead) of the Great War. Nor was the least effort made to copy, far less to conserve, the original structure; and what Watson finally came up with owes much more to the Brothers Grimm than anything in the Scottish vernacular. The Eilean Donan we see today has been described tactfully as 'a romantic reincarnation in the tradition of early twentieth-century castle revival' and – rather more bluntly – as a 'a rubbly Edwardian stage-set for life in the Middle Ages'.

And yet, with its turrets, portcullis and banqueting hall and – of course – its glorious views, Eilean Donan Castle (open to the public since 1955) has become a beloved tourist attraction: almost 320,000 people trooped over that bridge in 2012 alone. It has served as a set for innumerable films – from *Bonnie Prince Charlie* (1948), *Highlander* (1986) and the 1999 James Bond romp *The World Is Not Enough*. And not even Edinburgh Castle has been used more in adverts and on packaging, such being the splendour of Eilean Donan's setting.

The castle has been in the ownership of the Conchra Charitable Trust since 1983 and, since 1999 there has been a well-stocked visitor centre on the landward side of the bridge where you can buy untold goodies with a picture of Eilean Donan on them.

DID YOU KNOW?

The castle is said to be the most-photographed castle in the country, and is also noted as the most romantic castle of Scotland.

Eilean Donan is one of the only castles in the UK to feature a left-handed spiral staircase.

Legend has it that the castle is haunted by the ghost of a Spanish soldier, who was killed during the battle that took place at the castle in 1719.

The castle has appeared in a number of films over the years, such as the 1986 movie *Highlander* staring Sean Connery, and the 1999 James Bond film, *The World is Not Enough*.

05

GAELIC

Scottish Gaelic, according to the last census, in 2011, is spoken by almost 58,000 people (or about one Scot in a hundred) and is today a living, community language only in the Western Isles and some scattered pockets of the Inner Hebrides.

That is a far cry from the 231,594 speakers recorded in the census of 1881, when it was generally spoken everywhere north of the Highland Line and by 6.2 per cent of Scotland's population. Just at the edge of living memory, the language could be heard on the shores of Loch Lomond. In the late 1960s, native speakers survived in Arran and Perthshire, while the last in Aberdeenshire died only in 1985.

The main factor in its decline through the nineteenth century – there were almost 300,000 speakers (22.9 per cent of Scotland's population) in 1806 – was, of course, emigration, not least the infamous Clearances. This is dramatically attested by one startling figure: the 1901 total of 202,700 speakers of Gaelic and English in Scotland – and, across the ocean in Nova Scotia, some 100,000.

But the real and sustained fall is evident in the 1891 census onwards, reflecting the impact of the 1872 Education (Scotland) Act, which imposed English-medium lessons on schools everywhere. There were fewer than 100,000 speakers by 1981, and less than 70,000 by 1991 – hit further, by then, by the advent of television in the north-west from the late 1960s and, in very recent years, with the virtual colonisation of many Hebridean communities by English incomers.

It is a harsh fate for a Celtic language native to Scotland, whose roots are in Old Irish – the Gaels first began to colonise Dalriada (Argyll) in the sixth century – and which was spoken by every King of Scots until James IV fell at Flodden in 1513. The language survived in Galloway into the sixteenth century and, in one startling statistic, there are more Gaelic place names in Fife than there are on the Isle of Lewis (which, of course, came under heavy Norse settlement from late in the first millennium). Yet Gaelic is still denied recognition as an official language of either the United Kingdom or the European Union; Gaelic culture itself has been treated as second-class, alien and other in Scotland since the Battle of Harlaw in 1411, when Donald II, Lord of the Isles, was defeated in his bid for military domination of the northern mainland and, tacitly, the throne itself.

It is from this period we see the first denunciation of Highlanders as 'caterans' – freebooters; bandits: a few years earlier an Aberdeenshire priest, John of Fordun, had first articulated what are, even today, abiding prejudices:

Sorley MacLean (1911–96), our greatest Gaelic poet.

The Highlanders and people of the isles, however, are a savage and untamed race, rude and independent, given to rapine, ease-loving, clever and quick to learn, comely in person but unsightly in dress, hostile to the English people and language and, owing to this diversity of speech, even to their own nation.

They were also, he added primly, exceedingly cruel. The historic enemy of the Gael has been not the Englishman but the Lowland Scot and, even today, the cheap Glasgow press likes to mock backwards, drunken Sabbatarian 'teuchters'.

King James VI tried first to exterminate the people of Lewis – in a ridiculous 'plantation' project headed by the Fife Adventurers – and then, by the Statutes of Iona (commanding, for instance, southern education of their sons), to anglicise at least the clan chiefs. Later Stuarts had no aversion to raising Highland hosts in their bids to defend – and latterly to regain – the English throne; and the barbarities after the Battle of Culloden, in 1746, are well documented. Nor does the Church, even after the Reformation of 1560, emerge with much credit; only the Jacobite threat, from the late seventeenth century, inspired the most elementary provision of education, and there would not be a complete, far less affordable, Gaelic translation of the Bible until the nineteenth century.

Effective, as opposed to token, efforts to stem the haemorrhage can really be traced only to the 1960s, significantly as the Scottish National Party finally secured a permanent parliamentary bridgehead. The most important developments have been the belated adoption of Gaelic-medium primary education – the first unit opened at Breasclete on Lewis in 1986 – and such schooling is now widely available in the Highlands and Islands, with Gaelic-medium secondary education also on offer in Glasgow and Edinburgh. There has been significant funding for Gaelic television broadcasting since 1992, though little increase in real terms, and BBC Alba, a dedicated Gaelic television channel, was finally launched in the autumn of 2008.

There have been other, powerful forces against the night. The sweep of a new, evangelical religion across the Highlands and Hebrides from the late eighteenth century brought widespread Gaelic literacy and a confident Gaelic pulpit. Until the Second World War there was a lively Gaelic publishing industry, and An Comunn Gàidhealach and its annual National Mod has sustained interest in Gaelic song, some of the pre-war artistes being of extraordinarily high calibre.

In 1973, a new Gaelic folk-rock band, Runrig, seemed just another of the earnest little groups multiplying at the time, but by their 2018 retirement, the lads had won a considerable international following. Just in the nick of time, and as universal television broadcasting threatened to obliterate the distinctive culture of the north and west, Runrig made the ancient language rather cool.

Its greatest modern exponent, though, was the Gaelic poet and scholar Sorley MacLean, born on Raasay in 1911 and whose intense, urgent verse – to highly traditional lyrical metres but influenced by, for instance, John Dunne, Hugh MacDiarmid and even the Free Presbyterian pulpit – established that, even in the late twentieth century, the Gaelic language could powerfully address tormented love, socialist uprising or nuclear war.

There are some encouragements. Demand for Gaelic-medium teaching in Scotland's cities is rapidly growing and the fall in speakers recorded in 2011 was but marginal – with, in fact, a tiny increase in young people since 2001. The fear is that what was always a community tongue – of hearth and home, croft and sermon – is fast becoming a 'network' one; a language of self-conscious hobby, career or cultural diversion, less and less with each passing year a language of the heart.

Cum coin air iall.
Please keep dogs on a lead.

06

BAGPIPES

We do not know when the pipes reached Scotland and Ireland. There are no written references until the mid-sixteenth century, but what is striking from these records is that it was already an instrument of pomp, war and glory.

Pipers were prominent in battle. In every great household, the chief had a personal piper and these musicians would perform, for instance, at important funerals. In the Scottish Highlands, pipes were the stuff of nobility.

As an instrument, the bagpipe is not unique to Scotland. Until the sixteenth century, it was popular across Europe, usually the sort operated with underarm bellows. In modern times it survives in only a few isolated pockets, very much the folk instrument of shepherds and so on.

The Highland bagpipe consists of a chanter and three drones — at their grandest, these are handmade from African hardwood, trimmed with silver and iron and silk tassels — all attached to a sheepskin bag (usually encased in tartan or velvet), topped up with air by mouth and blow-pipe, and controlled otherwise by the piper's elbow.

The melody is fingered on the chanter — a double-reeded instrument in close kin to the oboe — and the three drones keep up a continuous chord. Constant air-pressure is essential for an even tone.

Black Watch pipers march in solemn procession during US President John F. Kennedy's funeral, November 1963.

There can, then, be no variations in volume and no pauses between notes.

It is all in the fingering of the chanter, and while the pipes are not difficult to learn they take many years to master, for their rhythm and song hinges on the most precise timing and the skilled use of grace-notes – some in extraordinarily complex arrangement.

There are limitations. The chanter has but a nine-note scale and, for instance, the modern 'Flower of Scotland', in all its mulish sentiment – the air has a 'flattened seventh' – cannot accurately be played on the pipes, though Scottish rugby internationals do witness heroic attempts.

The instrument must be precisely tuned: a piper of any standing will go to a great deal of trouble selecting and trimming reeds, and 'tune up' at length before any performance to steady – and settle – his

instrument. Great pipes can have long, long careers: at least one surviving set was played at Culloden.

By the mid-eighteenth century the pipes were used for relaxed merry-making in the typical Highland mansion – reels, jigs, strathspeys, slow airs, rendition of songs and so on. This popular fare is ceòl beag, 'light music'; far less accessible – but of great importance to your standing as a piper – is ceòl mòr, or piobaireachd (often pronounced 'pibroch' in English): music of much grander scale, elaborate in composition and demanding in the extreme.

A pibroch is of set pattern: begun with a slow theme (the ùrlar, or 'ground') followed by umpteen variations and concluding with the repetition of that theme. Most – this is the Highlands, after all – are laments; a particularly famous one, 'Lochaber No More', sounds so eerie that its performance was actually forbidden in Highland regiments during the Peninsular War, lest it ruin the morale of the troops. Another, 'Lament for the Children', is still performed at many Highland funerals.

Others are 'gatherings', or robust summons-to-arms pieces from a far-off and often brutal past. The marches with which the pipes are most popularly linked are overwhelmingly modern – from the early nineteenth century – and born of the instrument's long association with the British forces.

It is no coincidence that, over the past two centuries, scarcely any true pibroch has been created or generally accepted – perhaps, besides, because most now think the original principles of composition have been lost. There have been very successful new slow airs – of which 'The Sands of Kuwait', inspired by the first Gulf War in 1991, has been particularly popular.

What is striking about the original (and vast) body of pipe music is that until practically Victorian times not a note of it was written down. Through assorted schools (of which that of the MacCrimmons, pipers to the MacLeods of Dunvegan, is the most famous) pibrochs

Pipe Major Scott Taylor, of the 1st Battalion Black Watch, plays his bagpipes during a memorial for three lives lost in suicide attacks in Iraq.

were conveyed – and, indeed, probably composed – by mouth in a most sophisticated, syllabic language called canntaireachd, of which exponents survive to this day – notably Mrs Rona Lightfoot of South Uist. Canntaireachd captures even the most involved grace-notes in high detail and besides, through centuries, helped engrain even the most sophisticated pibroch accurately and in generational piping memory.

The instrument can be tremendous fun. (In recent years the Red Hot Chilli Pipers, in all their sexy swagger, have greatly augmented piping's appeal.) But the bagpipe – even at its simplest – can still indefinably command, order and inspire the Highland heart.

As someone sneered to a young Highland soldier, 'Whoever saw bagpipes in an orchestra?'

And as he very properly replied, 'Whoever saw a piano at the head of an army?'

GOLDEN EAGLE

This great soaring bird, of effortless flying abilities and cruel mien, is now all but unique to Scotland (though a tiny population hangs on in Cumbria, in north-west England).

It is huge – the biggest have a wingspan over seven feet and all have talons larger than the average fist – and it is scarce: only 440 breeding pairs are thought to survive. While a few eagles roam the skies in Dumfriesshire, the Highlands and Islands are today the eagle's main manor.

Shy and inordinately alert, you're unlikely to get close to one – an 'eagle' seen sitting on a fence post is invariably the much smaller buzzard – but keen eyes will spot them in majestic flight, readily identified by their sheer size and their extraordinary economy of motion.

The eagle is, of course, steeped in romance and lore, on the crest of armies and empires the world over and throughout the sweep of history. A Highland chief – head of a clan and bearing its arms – is entitled to wear three eagle feathers in his bonnet badge; a lesser chieftain can wear two. To the Druids, the eagle was the king of birds; to the Celts, it symbolised wisdom, indefatigability and great old age.

The birds are monogamous, tend to mate for life and are robustly territorial; a pair will usually take exclusive command of a given range, as big as 77 square miles. Eagles are – and with good reason – wary of people. They live far away from dwellings and favour heathery, treeless wastes over woodland.

Despite its logo, the name of Scotland's most famous hotel has nothing to do with eagles. It's a corruption of the Gaelic eglais – *a church – and refers to the chapel and well of Saint Mungo, which was restored as a memorial to the Haldane family owners of the Gleneagles estate.*

On the mainland they live at high altitude, but in the Hebrides – where, for complex reasons of climate, comparable conditions can be found very near sea level – they are often based near the coast.

Their nest, or eyrie – a great, twiggy affair – will be on the ledge of a cliff as inaccessible to man and beast as possible.

The female, oddly, tends to be bigger than the male; she will lay, typically, four eggs in the spring and incubate these for six weeks. On average, one or two chicks survive to fledge and float off to their own independent lives in the autumn. A very high proportion (up to 70 per cent) fail to survive their first winter, but, winning through to spring, an eagle may live for 20 years.

Golden eagles are not fussy eaters and, despite their ferocious reputation, will as happily dine on carrion as on anything warm, live and furry. Live prey can include grouse, rabbit, brown or blue hares, foxes, young deer and even – any port in a storm – the odd salmon, for one was found in a Lewis eyrie in 1961. They will, on occasion, seize young lambs. And once, a horrified gamekeeper had to fire a warning shot to save his terrified Jack Russell terrier, as it was hoisted audaciously into the air. (It was dropped, and survived, though for some weeks refused to go outdoors.)

It's an unusually quiet bird – the ominous cries and croaks in remote glens are invariably from ravens – and seems only to speak at all during the nesting season. For so mighty a bird, its infrequent vocals are oddly thin and pathetic, and have been described as 'puppy-like'.

They can be tamed, and excel at falconry; they are used to this day in Mongolia for hunting wolves. With no surviving predators in the wild, the main menace to golden eagles – historically and to this day – has been human persecution. They are still targeted by egg-collectors, eyries are often deliberately destroyed by irresponsible crofters, and there are still gamekeepers prepared to lay poisoned bait – all this despite the ferocious laws now protecting all our wild birds, and the eagle in particular. It has long been a criminal offence to visit an eyrie in use without a specific Scottish government permit.

The eagle survives, despite such nastiness and the loss of much habitat, because of its extraordinary skills; it's been grandly described as the 'pre-eminent diurnal hunter of medium-sized birds and animals in open country in the Northern Hemisphere'. Of all its hunting forays, a fifth successfully end in lunch, and virtually nothing escapes once contact is made – an eagle's terrifying talons can crunch at a pressure of 440 pounds per square inch. (That's 15 times stronger than the human hand.) The ferocity of the final attack – from both impact and the mighty braking snap of those huge wings – makes a bang comparable to a clap of thunder.

It is not, though, our only eagle species. Persecuted to extinction in Scotland before the First World War, Norwegian specimens of the white-tailed sea eagle were released in the Isle of Rum and elsewhere over a decade from 1975. More were let loose in Wester Ross in the 1990s and, from 2007, in Fife. These gigantic birds are now happily breeding and their numbers increase from year to year. You are most likely to see one by the Kylerhea ferry to Skye, where a pair have made their abode. Of close kin to the American bald eagle, their span can exceed eight feet and they feast largely on fish.

DID YOU KNOW?

....

Golden Eagles are monogamous, meaning that they keep the same mating partner throughout their lifetime. However, if one of the pair dies, the survivors have been known to readily accept a new mate!

....

The Golden Eagle is the eighth-most common bird depicted on postage stamps, with 155 known stamps issued to date.

....

For centuries, the Golden Eagle has been used in falconry, with the Eurasian subspecies used to hunt and kill dangerous prey such as Grey Wolves in some native communities.

....

The Golden Eagle can fly at average speeds of 28–32 mph.

....

Eagles feature prominently in Native American cultures. In most Native tribes, eagles are considered 'medicine birds', believed to possess magical healing powers.

....

35

MARY, QUEEN OF SCOTS

Centuries after her beheading, Mary, Queen of Scots continues to fascinate millions. But, though her meaningful, personal rule of Scotland lasted only six years, she was a grossly incompetent monarch.

Her real importance was her scarily strong claim to the throne of England. From the death of Mary Tudor in 1558, Mary Stuart was – by right and in law – its true queen, not Elizabeth I, conceived months before Henry VIII had got around to marrying her mother, and born while his first wife, Catherine of Aragon, was still living. Yet, as Mary I had gasped her last in 1558, she put her dynasty before her Catholicism. The crown passed to the Protestant wee sister, not the Queen of Scots.

Accordingly, for her entire life – largely as a pawn of others – Mary Stuart was the focus of dark politics, low diplomacy, innumerable conspiracies and some signally dreadful men. She spent her last two decades as a fuming prisoner in England until tricked into signing her name to a plot to kill her cousin. Her execution – that of an anointed sovereign, arrayed in the virtue-signalling red of a Roman Catholic martyr – sent shockwaves through Europe and even briefly reduced Elizabeth herself to paroxysms. Yet, entwined as their lives were and deeply as they fascinated each other – and whatever the contrivances of stage and screen in our time, such as the latest, eponymous 2019 film – the two women never, ever met.

There were other vulnerabilities. All her life Mary was prone to unexpected bouts of

Linlithgow Palace in West Lothian beautifully situated by Linlithgow Peel, is celebrated today as the birthplace of Mary, Queen of Scots.

mysterious, prostrating illness, which may have been the porphyria from which her son, James VI and I, certainly suffered and arguably stalked such descendants as George III and the Empress Frederick. This did little for Mary's credibility in an age loathe to see women in any position of authority, and when a monarch's personal vigour and valour meant much. And she was exceedingly unlucky in her men. Her first husband died within two years of their wedding, her second was a lout and her third scarce more than a psychopath.

Mary was born at Linlithgow Palace on 8 December 1542, and as his only surviving child inherited Scotland's throne when James V died six days later. She was also the great-niece of old, bloated Henry VIII (whose sister Margaret had been consort to James IV), and the infant's possibilities soon attracted his attention. Henry proposed her betrothal to his son, the future Edward VI of England, and, though this was at first reluctantly agreed, the

French (and a pro-French faction in Scotland) took violent exception. The result was the 'Rough Wooing,' as English forces made two wanton rampages through the Borders and into Edinburgh itself. But, by then, in August 1548, the five-year old Queen of Scots had been sent to France. A decade later she married the Dauphin Francis, heir to the French throne, which he ascended the following year, only to die of an ear-infection, still not seventeen, in December 1560. In August 1561 his widow arrived at Leith, near Edinburgh, to launch her personal reign.

Mary was no silly girl. She was a gifted correspondent, poet, horsewoman and seamstress. She enjoyed falconry, could play the lute and the virginals, and was fluent in French, Spanish, Italian, Latin and Greek – on top of English and her native Scots. By the standards of the age she was most attractive and, at five foot eleven inches, exceptionally tall. But she was obstinate, highly strung, lacked common sense, had scant understanding of the dark, fraught politics of Scotland and never bothered to learn Gaelic (then still the tongue of two-thirds of the land). She was far more interested in eventually succeeding Elizabeth than in getting to grips with the one realm that was actually hers to govern.

And few abroad could understand why she clung ostentatiously to her personal Catholicism in what, with sudden and near-totality, was now a Protestant realm. Nothing, too, could have infuriated Elizabeth I more than Mary's marriage to her cousin Henry Stuart, Lord Darnley in July 1565. As he was also a grandchild of Margaret Tudor (by her second marriage), it would only bolster the claims of any offspring to Elizabeth's throne.

This cynical match was Mary's ruin. Darnley was tall, boozy, vicious, vacuous and gay. By the following spring they loathed each other, and one awful night in March 1566, Darnley and assorted aristocratic thugs burst into the heavily pregnant Queen's chamber and hacked her Italian-born secretary, David Rizzio (himself possibly a notch on Darnley's bedpost), to death in front of her.

Her husband may have hoped to induce a fatal miscarriage. But Mary was delivered of the future James VI in June and was soon embroiled in plots to resolve the Darnley problem. His murder in February 1567 appalled Scotland's capital city, and Mary's tardiness in identifying and punishing his killers raised dark suspicion – capped when, only three months later (she arguably had little choice, as there is strong evidence he raped her) she married the Earl of Bothwell. Weeks later, Mary was overthrown and imprisoned on an island in Loch Leven, Kinross, where she miscarried tiny twins. She secured her escape in May 1568, only for her forces to be defeated days later at the Battle of Langside. Fleeing by sea, she finally, fatefully, ordered landing in England, where

she spent the rest of her life under house-arrest with assorted, embarrassed Protestant nobles.

Her entrapment and execution now seem pointlessly vindictive. By 1587 Mary was beyond childbearing age, loathed in Scotland, despised in England and a threat to no one. Her judicial murder only invited the Spanish Armada.

Yet, from the accession of her son to the English throne in 1603, all our monarchs ever since have been her descendants. As Mary herself once poignantly put it, 'In my end is my beginning.'

Statue of Mary, Queen of Scots in a park beside Linlithgow Palace.

09

EDINBURGH CASTLE

So splendid is Edinburgh Castle that one could happily lose an entire day in the place. And it has long been Scotland's most popular paid visitor attraction, winning more than a million annual visitors.

It's partly the treasures, partly the outlook – but it is mostly because it's the most archetypal castle any child could imagine: lofty battlements, great guns, rugged chambers, armed soldiers and even a drawbridge.

Its utterly commanding position over the city – atop the solidified lava 'plug' of an extinct volcano – attests both to Edinburgh's dramatic geology and the near-certainty (the site being so high and so dominant) of human fortification of some sort or other since at least the second century AD. Its

earliest appearance in written history is in AD 600, when we learn of Mynyddog, king of the Brythonic kingdom of Gododdin, or south-east Scotland.

To make matters more confusing still, Mynyddog the 'Brython', in Scotland, was ethnically Welsh; place names of Welsh origin are in Lothian to this day. Nor did he last very long, for the war-band he dispatched to fight invading Angles was all but wiped out and, in AD 638, these Germanic settlers successfully besieged his capital, Din Eidyn.

Dùn Èideann is the Scottish Gaelic name to this day for fort and city, and it has even been transplanted to New Zealand: Dunedin is the second-biggest city on the South Island. But the Angles won, and the Scottish city – initially as part of the kingdom of Northumbria – has been Edinburgh ever since. It seems rather too late to do anything about it now.

Nor has Edinburgh ever entirely shed wider Scottish suspicions that it is in truth part of England, even though Lothian was finally recovered by an emerging, independent Scotland in the tenth century. Oddly enough, it would be only after the murder in 1437 of King James I, in Perth, that Edinburgh became Scotland's capital and the seat of her monarch.

But history had already swirled atop her Castle Rock for centuries and would do so for centuries more; even today, this is still a working military base where local police enjoy no jurisdiction.

Edinburgh grew outwards from the Castle Rock, and the walled city of the Middle Ages centred on the 'Old Town', which straggles down the tail of the crag as first the Lawnmarket, then the High Street, the Canongate and – at its foot – the Royal Palace of Holyrood House, still the Queen's only official residence in Scotland and where she spends some time every summer. In all, it's one illustrious street known as the Royal Mile.

By the reign of Malcolm III – a well-meaning but illiterate Highlander – Edinburgh enjoyed

The firing of the One O'Clock Gun dates back to 1861 when it allowed ships in the Firth of Forth to set the maritime clocks they needed to navigate the world's oceans.

its first serious run as a royal court and the oldest building in the city – the tiny St Margaret's Chapel, erected early in the twelfth century – commemorates his rather ghastly wife, who did her best to anglicise the kingdom and succeeded in dethroning the Celtic Church for Roman Catholicism.

Three of her sons, in succession, became King of Scots and David I – reigning from 1124 to 1153 – built the first serious castle at Edinburgh, little of which would survive the Wars of Independence: Robert the Bruce himself, four months before his triumph at Bannockburn, ordered the demolition of its defences after his doughtiest men overwhelmed the English garrison in a night attack.

Edinburgh Castle would be besieged a good few times thereafter, and with occasional success; in 1745, the dreadful old Hanoverian, General Preston, successfully resisted Charles Edward Stuart's rough wooing, callously bombarding the city (and citizenry) with his cannon until a Jacobite blockade was lifted – and then even after it was.

Within these walls, the first king of all Britain's realms, James VI and I, was born in 1566. In 1633, Charles I would be the last to sleep here. In 1707, following the Articles of Union, the old Crown Jewels (the Honours of Scotland) were locked away in a sealed apartment, till folk thought they were lost entirely; they were rediscovered in February 1818 by a search party, authorised by the Prince Regent and led by Sir Walter Scott.

That was the start, really, of the castle's more peaceful role as a tourist attraction. The Crown, Sword and Sceptre have been on display ever since, save for the interruption of the Second World War and the castle's most recent dark note in history – as plans recovered following the war made clear, Nazi Germany had earmarked it as their Scottish

Massed Pipes and Drums performing in the annual Edinburgh Military Tattoo.

headquarters come the invasion of Britain and the occupation of Scotland.

The castle did, indeed, serve as a prison for the odd captured Luftwaffe pilot, and during the Great War one noisy 'Red Clydesider', David Kirkwood, had been briefly jailed there … by Hitler's war, he was a respected Labour MP.

Most of the Edinburgh Castle you see today – such as the Half-Moon Battery and the Portcullis Gate – dates from 1573, when substantial rebuilding began after a massive bombardment and the final surrender of William Kirkcaldy of Grange, who had held out from 1571 in doughty support of the exiled Mary, Queen of Scots. (He was speedily hanged.)

Much was added besides in Victorian times and the One O'Clock Gun, an extraordinary city custom, has boomed daily from these battlements since 1861. And a far older piece of artillery, Mons Meg – a belated 1457 wedding present from Burgundy for

King James II and his Burgundian bride – is on proud display at the castle, though firmly retired since 1681, after her barrel burst while booming salute to the future James VII and II. (And she's been kept safely inside since the early 1980s.)

Other glories here include the solemn Scottish National War Memorial, the absorbing Scottish National War Museum, the old crown jewels (joined, only in 1996, by the Stone of Destiny, on which British monarchs are crowned at Westminster Abbey), St Margaret's Chapel and even a little cemetery where garrisoned soldiers have long buried their pets.

All over Edinburgh, the castle seems to loom on the skyline from all sorts of unexpected angles. Every summer on its Esplanade, since 1950, it hosts the Military Tattoo, a nightly display of Scottish military skill, glamour, derring-do and skirling pipes.

All that aside, it is well worth visiting Edinburgh Castle simply for the views from it – they are wonderful.

10

JOHN KNOX

John Knox was the father of Presbyterianism, the founder of a distinct and abiding sense of the Scottish nation, and the first man in history to call for free, universal education.

Yet of all the sermons he preached, only two survive. Scarcely any monuments stand to Knox's memory in Scotland. And his unmarked grave lies beneath an Edinburgh car park. For decades indeed he has been generally vilified.

John Knox was born around 1514 in Haddington, East Lothian, and in 1529 he went to study for the priesthood at the University of St Andrews. Though ordained in 1536, he worked not as a clergyman but (briefly) as a lawyer, then as a jobbing tutor of the sons of minor gentry. But he was fast caught up in the building crisis in his country at that time: the

mounting popular revulsion at the state of the Church, and its pomp and power in the land.

Even by medieval standards, the Roman Catholic Church in Scotland was extraordinarily corrupt, owning more than half of Scotland's land and enjoying 18 times as much revenue as the Crown. Monasteries and convents were notoriously debauched and more than a quarter of all the country's illegitimate children were the progeny of priests. Expectations of clergy were low.

With its considerable trade over the North Sea to Europe, Lutheran literature began increasingly

John Knox's house in Edinburgh's High Street, now a museum and popular tourist attraction.

to circulate in Scotland and, as new ideas took hold – for instance, that the Scriptures be translated into Scots and that everyone be taught to read them; that the monasteries be disbanded; that the worship of statues and relics be overthrown – the authorities tried increasingly to repress them. Patrick Hamilton, a convert to Protestantism and a persuasive preacher, was burned at the stake in 1528, but his martyrdom served only to dignify and expand the cause.

About this time, Knox himself was converted and joined the ranks of another preacher, George Wishart, both as colleague and bodyguard. However, in 1546 Cardinal Beaton, Archbishop of St Andrews (who, among other debauches, had sired ten bastard children), had Wishart seized, strangled and burned. In response, furious Protestant nobles stormed Beaton's castle, and slew and mutilated him. For a time, under general French siege, the Protestants held St Andrews and a tearful Knox was prevailed upon to serve as their minister. Then, in 1547, the city fell; some were slammed in prison and others (including Knox) put to wretched service as slaves in French galleys. It was 19 long months before he was freed.

Knox then spent five years in England, his reputation growing all the while as a preacher, and made his first marriage to Margery Bowes, who bore him two sons. On the accession of Mary I (determined to restore England to Catholicism), they prudently escaped to the Continent.

There, in Geneva, he met John Calvin, the brilliant Frenchman who had, from comprehensive study of the Bible alone, hammered out not only a comprehensive Reformed theology but a whole new order of society. The city, Knox later remarked, was 'the most perfect school of Christ that was ever on earth since the days of the apostles'.

He was less content during his time in Frankfurt, but back home Protestantism was remorselessly advancing. In 1555, its leaders, the 'Lords of the Congregation', invited Knox back to his native land to preach. He toured about for nine months before continued disorder and persecution forced him back to Geneva.

There, he wrote polemical pamphlets. The most notorious is his *The First Blast of the Trumpet Against the Monstrous Regiment of Women*; it had, in both Mary Tudor and Mary of Guise, perfectly legitimate targets, but it infuriated Mary's successor, Elizabeth I, who might otherwise have been much more kindly disposed to his coherent and biblical faith.

In his *Appellations to the Nobility and Commonality of Scotland*, he extended to ordinary people the right – indeed, the duty – to rebel against wicked and despotic rulers: as Knox would later tell Mary, Queen of Scots (they had several uncomfortable audiences), 'The sword of justice is God's, and if princes and rulers fail to use it, others may.' The moral right to overthrow tyranny is now universally accepted; in the sixteenth century, this was an extraordinary new idea.

Knox was able to return to Scotland permanently in 1559, the most charismatic and compelling (if not the most learned) of the land's Reformed preachers. Within days of his arrival, a passionate sermon at St John's in Perth brought widespread uprising against Roman Catholic superstition – the overthrow of religious houses, the destruction of images and idols. And that June he became minister of Edinburgh. You can still see his pulpit in the High Kirk of St Giles.

With the Treaty of Berwick the following year, both the English and the French agreed to leave Scotland and the Reformation was complete. Parliament now directed Knox and five colleagues to draw up the creeds of what was not just a new Kirk but a new society; within months, they had completed a Confession of Faith, outlining Christian doctrine; a Book of Common Order, setting forth rules for public worship; and the *First Book of Discipline*, in many ways very modern. It set out, for instance, sensible rules for public sanitation; care for the poor; that schools in every parish should be free to all, for both boys and girls, and funded by the wealth of the overthrown Catholic order. (Knox was frustrated in this: the nobility gobbled up most of the lands and money.)

Margery's death late in 1560 was an undoubted blow, but in 1564 Knox married again – an eyebrow-raising match not just because his new bride, Margaret Stewart, was of noble birth (the daughter of Andrew Stewart, 2nd Lord Ochiltree, and a distant cousin of the Queen) but because Knox was 50 and she was only 17. Yet it seems to have been a true love match – he sent fond notes to his 'Dearlibelovit' – and they would have three daughters.

Knox wrote another book, *The History of the Reformation in Scotland*, and preached and preached, typically spending half an hour 'opening' the text

before applying it (and with vigour) to the immediate Scottish situation of the hour, increasingly against the Queen. He was repeatedly summoned to account for himself to her, and courteously attended, but refused to be told what he could and could not preach. Such was his following that she never dared to strike him down. Eventually, of course, she destroyed herself, and it was Knox who preached the sermon at the coronation of the infant James VI, and somehow maintained his ministry through the ensuing years of tumult and civil war.

John Knox died peacefully in his bed in Edinburgh on 24 November 1572, just three weeks after handing over St Giles to his successor. By his open grave, Scotland's new Regent, James Douglas, 4th Earl of Morton, pronounced soberly: 'There lies he, who never feared the face of man.'

The sculpted Reformation Wall celebrating the fathers of the Reformation in Geneva's Parc Des Bastions which includes John Knox.

11

BEN NEVIS

At 4,409 feet tall – that's 1,344 metres – Ben Nevis is the highest mountain not just in Scotland but in all the British Isles… though she had to wait till 1847, and new surveying technology, before that could definitively be confirmed.

Majestic as she is, she is on no account to be trifled with. Her very name, in Gaelic – Beinn Nibheis – almost certainly means 'Mount Malignant'. Benign and round she may appear on a sunny Lochaber day, and though climbed annually by around 100,000 people, several die on Ben Nevis every year, by avalanche, tumble or exposure. The north and west faces of the mountain are vertiginous, terrible cliffs – some a sheer drop of 2,300 feet, among the highest on mainland Britain. Even in high summer, chill snow remains here and there in the crevices.

April is said to be the best month – the air is clearest and there is least likelihood of cloud at the top – and the tramp up will take a fit adult about

Three-quarters of all who climb Ben Nevis ascend by the crude track from Achintee Farm in lower Glen Nevis, still foolishly described as the 'tourist route', as if one could strut up it in T-shirt and trainers. In fact it's a rough, eroded, stony trek, making short work of shoddy shoes – anyone attempting the Ben should dress appropriately and take all sensible precautions. As the accomplished mountaineer W. H. Murray wrote in 1960: 'Thirty three people have been killed on this mountain in the last eight years. Three important things to remember about Nevis are its height, its isolation, and its site on the west coast. Its summit lies close to the level of perpetual snow and right in the storm track of the North Atlantic hurricanes, so that weather conditions vary with extreme speed. The summit has an average of two hundred and sixty-one gales each year, and no other mountain breaks the blow when a storm strikes. Hurricanes exceeding one hundred miles an hour blow not only annually but, in winter, often laden with snow, and they gust up to a hundred and fifty miles an hour. For these reasons the mountain is dangerous …'

three and a half hours, allowing another two for the descent and keeping, all the while, a most cautious eye on the weather.

The first record we have of ascent was by James Robertson, an Edinburgh botanist, on 17 August 1771. John Keats managed the climb in 1818, joking afterwards that it was like 'mounting ten St Pauls without the convenience of a staircase'.

Thereafter, for certain rugged men in late Victorian times, Ben Nevis became – briefly – almost domestic.

Through the summers of two successive years – 1881 and 1882 – one Clement Wragge, an English scientist, climbed the mountain every day, regardless of conditions, for weather observation and recording. He was mocked, inevitably, as 'Inclement Wragge', but it was largely on his account that in 1883 an observatory was built at the summit, with a path and little bridges laid to it. It was joined by a tiny 'hotel' – hostel would be more apt – and they even enjoyed a direct telephone connection to Fort William.

That kept young Andrew Miller – a schoolmate of Donald MacCulloch's in the golden years early in the twentieth century – rather busy, for his father owned the lofty, if tiny, bunkhouse and, as MacCulloch recalled:

[Andrew] thought nothing of climbing Ben Nevis twice in one day, not for pleasure but of necessity. He said, 'It was quite common for me to take something up to the hotel in the morning then, after returning home, a telephone message would come in the afternoon saying that they had run out of some food, such as butcher meat, owing to the arrival of an unexpected number of climbers.' It took him about two hours to get to the top of the Ben and he cut this time by about thirty minutes on the way down …

The observatory, though, closed in 1904 after the withdrawal of government funding, and both structures had been demolished by the autumn of 1913. Two years earlier, on 16 May 1911 and in his Ford Tourer, one Henry Alexander of Edinburgh had managed to make the first ascent by motorcar.

The Ben Nevis Hill Race seems to have been first held in 1895 and after a long hiatus from 1903 was revived in 1937. The current record for the run to the top and back – 1 hour, 25 minutes and 34 seconds – was set by Kenny Stuart, of Keswick Athletic Club, in 1984.

In 2000 the Ben Nevis Estate was bought by the John Muir Trust, a Scottish conservation charity. Controversy continues over careless, ill-equipped visitors; the propriety of safety-aids at or near the top for the lost – such as posts to mark the safe path down in thick mist; and litter and detritus left at the summit, from the spectacular discovery in 2006 of a piano under a cairn (carried up as a stunt in the

decades before) to the disconcerting practice of scattering cremated human remains.

Safely shod, wisely clad and granted sunshine, one's reward on attaining the summit is a view of a great sea of peaks, glens and islands – from Ben Lomond to Torridon; from the Cairngorms to the Outer Hebrides. In exceptional conditions, one can even see the distant hills of Ireland.

'[Ben Nevis] has not the dramatic appearance of the sharp-peaked Alps or even the Cuillin of Skye … Its massive bulk, its rounded contours and wide-flowing skirts give it a venerable appearance, like an aged law-lord sitting in judgement. This comparison is even more pronounced when the Ben is clad in the regal colours of autumn and the early snows have draped his broad shoulders with an ermine cape.'
Donald B. MacCulloch, *Romantic Lochaber*, 1971

DID YOU KNOW?

On 17 August 1771, botanist James Robinson from Edinburgh became the first recorded person to reach the summit of Ben Nevis.

In 2006, a group of volunteers from the John Muir Trust found the remains of a piano buried at the summit. The piano is thought to have been carried up the mountain to raise money for charity, over 20 years earlier.

Over 100,000 tourists from across the world visit Ben Nevis each year.

It's not just people who've reached the top of Ben Nevis. In 1911 a Model T Ford was driven up the mountain and in 1981 a group of students pushed a bed up to the summit to raise money for charity.

12

TARTAN

Nothing so embodies Scottishness – at home and overseas – as tartan: vivid, chequered cloth, usually in fine wool and (thanks to modern dyes) occasionally in vivid hues.

And no fabric in the world has such élan in all its rich associations – majestic, misted landscape; close-knit community; military heroism (as recently as 1940, Highland regiments still wore the kilt to battle: the awed Germans during the Great War dubbed these gutsy fighters the 'Ladies from Hell'); and, being Scottish, lost causes, last stands and forlorn hopes.

Nor, surely, has any cloth been the stuff of more specious nonsense. Only two centuries ago, tartan was, in wider Scottish thought, the scruffy raiment of ignorant Highlanders. For 36 panicked years, it was – by full force of law – actually banned.

In truth, specific patterns of tartan – 'setts' – were never identified with particular clans, far less exclusive surnames. Rather, they were associated with regions, the hue and arrangement reflecting such skills and colourings as might be locally available.

And despite assorted Royal Mile signs proclaiming IF YOUR NAME IS HERE, WE HAVE YOUR TARTAN – you can still see, in high summer, knots of anxious tourists clustered about them – you can wear any sett you like. There is no authority with any force in Scots law able to cart you away in irons for popping up at a bash in a blaze of colour to which you are not

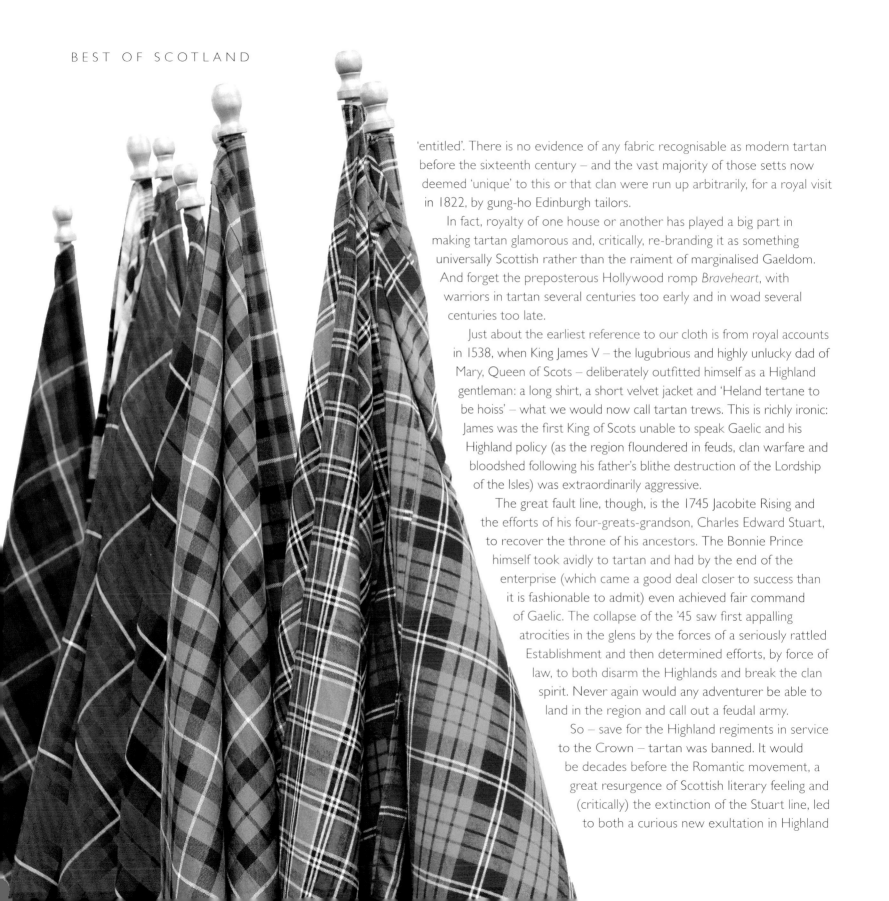

'entitled'. There is no evidence of any fabric recognisable as modern tartan before the sixteenth century – and the vast majority of those setts now deemed 'unique' to this or that clan were run up arbitrarily, for a royal visit in 1822, by gung-ho Edinburgh tailors.

In fact, royalty of one house or another has played a big part in making tartan glamorous and, critically, re-branding it as something universally Scottish rather than the raiment of marginalised Gaeldom. And forget the preposterous Hollywood romp *Braveheart*, with warriors in tartan several centuries too early and in woad several centuries too late.

Just about the earliest reference to our cloth is from royal accounts in 1538, when King James V – the lugubrious and highly unlucky dad of Mary, Queen of Scots – deliberately outfitted himself as a Highland gentleman: a long shirt, a short velvet jacket and 'Heland tertane to be hoiss' – what we would now call tartan trews. This is richly ironic: James was the first King of Scots unable to speak Gaelic and his Highland policy (as the region floundered in feuds, clan warfare and bloodshed following his father's blithe destruction of the Lordship of the Isles) was extraordinarily aggressive.

The great fault line, though, is the 1745 Jacobite Rising and the efforts of his four-greats-grandson, Charles Edward Stuart, to recover the throne of his ancestors. The Bonnie Prince himself took avidly to tartan and had by the end of the enterprise (which came a good deal closer to success than it is fashionable to admit) even achieved fair command of Gaelic. The collapse of the '45 saw first appalling atrocities in the glens by the forces of a seriously rattled Establishment and then determined efforts, by force of law, to both disarm the Highlands and break the clan spirit. Never again would any adventurer be able to land in the region and call out a feudal army.

So – save for the Highland regiments in service to the Crown – tartan was banned. It would be decades before the Romantic movement, a great resurgence of Scottish literary feeling and (critically) the extinction of the Stuart line, led to both a curious new exultation in Highland scenery and a new view of Highlanders themselves: a people picturesque, heroic and gallant.

Central to this was Sir Walter Scott, whose ripping yarns and stylised weepies became colossal bestsellers. And one important fan was King George IV, who in 1822 made a very grand visit to Edinburgh – the first reigning monarch to set foot in Scotland since 1650. Once it became known that His Majesty was to appear in the kilt, everybody who was anybody dashed to order yards of tartan.

Sir Walter stage-managed the occasion and Sir Henry Raeburn dashed off all sorts of commemorative paintings. (The one of the very fat and really rather nutty king himself was less than candid: Raeburn's idealised portrait removed several stones of Hanoverian blubber and recorded neither his monarch's flesh-coloured stockings nor that his kilt had been rather too short.)

More importantly, scores of new tartans were simply invented for the gaudy pageant – not least by two eccentric brothers, the 'Sobieski Stuarts', who claimed to be grandsons of the Bonnie Prince. There followed several pompous illustrated books (indeed, the Sobieski Stuarts published the most influential, the *Vestiarium Scoticum*) giving these patterns venerable (but entirely false) provenance.

The whole racket was gloriously capped by George IV's niece, Queen Victoria, and her Albert, who in 1848 acquired the Balmoral Estate, replaced its cramped mansion with a

Queen Victoria and Prince Albert put tartan at the forefront of fashion in the mid-nineteenth century and after buying Balmoral as a gift for his wife, Albert had the interior redesigned almost wholly with tartans.

great Germanic heap and decorated its interior with tartan abandon. They (and their estate employees) wore the fabric throughout their long Scottish holidays (and, to this day, the Queen's menfolk still don the kilt for any function in or north of Perth). The industry has never looked back.

The great irony is that even as Victoria and her household played out their Highland idyll, terrible things were happening to her Highland subjects in the real world: the outfitting of Balmoral coincided with the worst of the Clearances.

The Queen herself, blind to such horrors and with not the least sense of irony, once absurdly cooed in company, 'I myself am a Jacobite at heart.'

And yet … from a land so damp and dreich in many ways, it is hard not to warm to our happy begetting of a textile so cheerful and a brand so brilliant; or to the sight, at clan gatherings and Years of Homecoming, of the arrival of so many of the Scots diaspora, generations removed from their ancestral land, of Highland name and American or Antipodean habit, stirred and enthusing in the plaid of their forebears.

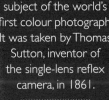

13

RED DEER

The red deer, *cervus elaphus*, is Britain's largest wild mammal and is found, these days – after centuries of retreat – largely on the moors and mountains of Scotland.

And, thanks to Edwin Landseer's celebrated painting of a stag in all its hauteur, it's perhaps our most iconic animal.

In the twenty-first century, there are also a great many of them. It's far from easy to count an animal so fleet and elusive, but in 2011 there were reckoned to be 350,000 red deer in the UK, with at least 300,000 in Scotland. And it is becoming a serious problem, not just because their feeding habits damage forestry and crops but because, as they move with increasing boldness on the margins of towns and cities, they are causing more and more road accidents.

This is scarcely the beast's fault. Since Victorian times, Highland estates have done very nicely out of deer-stalking; and gentry paying great sums for a week's sport naturally want to bump off handsome trophy-headed stags.

To keep a given population in balance, the hinds must then be culled by estate staff each autumn and, with fewer of these tweeded servants than there used to be – and a British market that remains stubbornly suspicious of venison – this is not, nationally, done with efficiency.

Nor have millennia of human war on their predators helped: the lynx and the bear have long been extinct, and the last Scottish wolf bought it in the eighteenth century. (Indeed, wolves were once such a problem that many Highland communities buried their dead on small islands – starving wolves were not particular – and, as late as 1549, Archdeacon Donald Monro, in an important description of the Western Isles, related of Harris, as an evident selling-point, 'there are no wolves there'.)

Southern deer – Scotland's main population is in Dumfriesshire – favour the woodland life, but the deer of the Highlands have, of necessity, adapted to the open braes and, in summer, roam very high. They are significantly smaller than their fatted forest cousins and hinds may take three years to attain sexual maturity; a woodland hind typically bears her first calf in her second year.

The sociology of red deer is complex and was the subject of exhaustive study by Frank Fraser Darling and others. Woodland deer tend to live on their lonesome, or as mother-and-child combinations. Mountain deer tend to form large, loose herds, though – save for the 'rut', or mating season – only with their own sex.

The rut begins in late September, runs to November, and is a stark Darwinian business. A randy stag has a distinctive and faintly chilling roar – a primal sound in the Highland autumn – and, as they stomp back to the ladies, stags engage in much strutting, showmanship and – if necessary – dreadful fights, occasionally to the death and invariably to some injury, for the right to mate. (Indeed, a rutting stag will even attack a human; in 2011, a hapless gentleman was charged – and sent flying – in London's Bushy Park; and there was a still more horrific attack on a woman in Lochaber late in 2013. So give them a respectful distance.)

The dominant stag then mates exclusively with the available hinds; but, next year, he has to do battle all over again, and even the greatest and most ferocious male will finally be deposed.

The Monarch of the Glen is an oil painting by the English painter Sir Edwin Landseer. It was commissioned as part of three panels to hang in the Houses of Parliament but is now part of the Scottish National Gallery collection.

Red deer like grasses and sweet young shrubs – such as heather and bilberry – but will gnaw on forest shoots in a tight winter. A stag's antlers are bone – not horn – and are shed every spring; whereon a fresh head-set starts to grow from new velveted buds. (Where the local diet is lacking in calcium, a stag will often cheerfully eat his discarded old ones.)

The older a stag, the more elaborate and magnificent his antlers will be: a 'royal' will sport ten 'points' – that is, five on each – and in full and mature splendour as many as sixteen.

Exceptionally, red deer can live to eighteen or so. There is heavy infant mortality and many young beasts, on the hill, perish in their first winter.

There are other species of deer in Scotland, though only the dainty little roe (there are 800,000 of them) is likewise native. The sika deer, of classic fairy-tale appearance, was introduced to a Fife estate in 1870; they are now widely established and there is some interbreeding with the red. In 1952, some reindeer were brought from Sweden to the Cairngorms and, today, the 150-strong herd of these gentle animals is quite an attraction.

Venison is a delicious, high-protein meat and is at last increasingly available in supermarkets – especially as red deer are now reared on a few commercial farms. Like all game, it is very low in fat and your seasoned joint should be rubbed well with butter or duck-fat, flown through a very hot oven – half an hour to 40 minutes, reducing the heat after 20 and perhaps tossing a glass of red wine into the pan – and then wrapped in foil and allowed to rest for another 20 minutes. This will give pink, succulent meat. Alternatively, steaks or 'collops' can be flash-fried in a pan, the juices perhaps finished off with stock, whisky and cream.

DID YOU KNOW?

In Roman times, red deer were used to pull coaches in the festivals related to the worship of goddess Diana, the goddess of hunting.

There are a few subspecies of red deer in which the stags grow mane of hair around their neck during the autumn season. This gives them a very regal look.

The largest species is the Caspian Red Deer, while the smallest species is the Corsican Red Deer.

Male red deer are known as stags and females of the species are called hinds.

The red deer has featured as the subject of many paintings. Differing in style from Landseer's *Monarch of the Glen* masterpiece, Franz Marc's 1913 Cubist work, *Red Deer*, captures the delicate grace and strength of the animal, using simple shapes and colours.

<u>14</u>

HAGGIS

Laws are like sausages, runs an old adage in American politics: they're good to have, but you don't want to watch them being made.

And, even by the gory standards of global charcuterie, making Scotland's most famous national dish – from scratch – is not for the faint-hearted.

The classic ingredients for a haggis are a sheep's 'pluck and bag': that is, the beast's stomach, in which a large festive-sized haggis is encased (for smaller haggis, bits of intestine are used, though many today are encased in ignoble plastic) and, hauled forth as one mass, its heart, liver and lungs. These inner organs are boiled (steam wheezing mournfully through the forlorn windpipe, hanging over the edge of the pan) and, once cool, are minced or grated.

They're then mixed with toasted oatmeal, suet, finely chopped onion and seasoning – butchers tend to be very precious about their given 'secret formula',

but it's typically salt, pepper and mace. All this is at last stuffed into the bag, which is sewn or clipped shut, and steamed as one. Cometh the hour, the haggis is (for the third time) cooked and served, classically with 'mashit neeps an' bashit tatties' – mashed swede and potato.

That said, there are assorted variants, the stuff of murmured and at times bitter rivalry between the nation's butchers – many of whom enter the annual competition to see who, in a given year, can make the best one. Some add bacon, or lamb stock, or touches of exotic seasoning such as coriander. When it emerged that the winner one year had made his haggis with pork fat, there was dark talk as to the dish's final authenticity.

A Burns Supper is a night to celebrate the life and works of the national Bard, Rabbie Burns. It can range from a casual gathering to a formal dinner with generous servings of pomp and circumstance. 'The Selkirk Grace' is usually recited in Scots to usher in the meal, before the star attraction, the Haggis, is piped in. The address will follow, with Burns's 'To a Haggis' read out to rapturous applause. The haggis is cut open to great cheer and a toast is made: The Haggis!

the menu of every respectable local chippie.

And we seem to be eating more of it than ever. In the early 1990s MacSween of Edinburgh – whose tasty version, notable for generous use of pinhead oatmeal and a lovely nubbly texture, is widely available in Scottish supermarkets – made about 200 tonnes a year. By 2006, it was 700. A ten-pound 'Chieftain' haggis is churned out in January for every other golf club's Burns Supper and most Scottish butchers that month find themselves making it in great quantities every day, such is the demand.

But – when the

It may come as a genuine surprise to be assured that haggis is quite delicious – warm, filling winter fare, as good as giving yourself a hug. It is also remarkably good for you: a nutritionally balanced meal replete with protein and fibre. And haggis is something Scots eat in enormous quantity – and not just at the great national feasts, St Andrew's Day (30 November) or Burns Night (25 January). For many Scottish families, it is a regular on the table. Haggis, meanwhile, sliced and deep-fried, is on

seasoning has been applied with a light hand – haggis can be a useful handmaiden to other dishes. In recent years 'Balmoral chicken' – supremes or fillets of fowl stuffed with juicy haggis – has become rather a staple of Scottish restaurants, typically with a whisky-based sauce. There are such curious Scots-Indian variants as haggis pakora, and cookery writer Sue Lawrence has even published a heroic recipe for haggis lasagne. One Scottish enterprise even sells haggis, ready to warm and serve, in a tin.

The people of Orkney even indulge in the splendidly named 'hagshot pie' – filled with haggis and topped with 'clapshot', a swede and tattie mix.

And then there is the issue of export. Scots overseas are desperate for an occasional haggis fix – no easy matter in, say, the United States, which bans the import of all meat products. While there are tales of nefarious smuggling, most cook it up locally. Though there is another way round the problem: MacSween in the early 1980s invented a surprisingly popular vegetarian haggis, fat with nuts, lentils and beans.

There is one abiding national joke, for which more tourists than might care to admit regularly fall: that the haggis is, in fact, a wild animal. The gullible are further assured that the legs on one side are longer than the other, the better to skip around the sides of craggy Scottish mountains.

Certainly innumerable comic postcards are sold on this theme, and Christie's of Bruntsfield – one of Edinburgh's most respected butchers – is not above playing on it. Its window often boasts the sly sign, 'HAGGIS – freshly shot'.

15

HARRIS TWEED

Harris Tweed, *an clo mor* – the 'Great Cloth' – is up there with Shantung silk, Egyptian cotton and cashmere as one of the greatest fabrics in the world.

Redolent of Hebridean romance, stately homes, rough shooting, gracious living, the joys of rod and gun and hill and river, and generally the gentry, all the more indeed on account of that lived-in, beloved old jacket, the draughtiness of their residences and the amount of lead in their game.

Very little Harris Tweed is now made on Harris proper. Yet it was there, in about 1840, by one version, that the tough, home-spun, handwoven cloth first caught the eye of its new owner, the Earl of Dunmore, who decided to have acres of his own Murray tartan woven in the stuff for his local retainers.

By another account it was in 1851, when Lady Dunmore finally deigned to visit her man's Hebridean redoubt, that she was so taken by the weaving of two sisters, Marion and Christina MacLeod, that she sent them off on a short course to Paisley to learn still better techniques. The 'Paisley Sisters' are still proudly remembered on Harris and their roofless cottage, hard by the shore in the village of Strond, still stands.

What we do know is that the Dunmores not only encouraged their posh friends to order this 'Harris Tweed' but besides won the interest of city merchants. And if there was a profound irony in

the timing – Harris Tweed was marketed expressly for its charm as a home-woven peasant product, even as the wider British textiles industry became overwhelmingly mechanised – there was also profound luck. Queen Victoria and her Albert had acquired Balmoral, gone in avidly for tweed and tartan, and suddenly made Highland estates (or at least Highland holidays) very fashionable.

But it was Lewis – and especially the merchants of Stornoway – who took fast command of the operation, and most Harris Tweed has long been made on that island. For many years, the principal market was the British landed class and the tens of thousands they employed – the cloth soon became the only thing proper for outfitting your ghillies, gamekeepers and so on. When that world went into precipitous decline after the Kaiser's War, a new market emerged and stood for decades: the millions of dashing American men whose desire was a Harris Tweed 'sports coat'.

There was big money in the cloth, and all sorts of cheats have occurred over the years, from a sweatshop factory unmasked in London to villages in the shadier parts of the Far East deliberately changing their name to Harris.

Island weavers struggled to cope with demand, and by the 1930s some deft solution had to be found to break serious bottlenecks in production without compromising the brand. To make a long story short, early-stage production (carding, spinning and dyeing of the yarn itself) was mechanised; it was decreed that the use of any pure 'virgin' (i.e. not recycled)

With new, clever marketing strategies targeting top fashion designers, Harris Tweed Hebrides' customers include Alexander McQueen, Chanel, YSL, Paul Smith and Vivienne Westwood, whose beautifully tailored suit is on display at the National Museum of Scotland.

wool was acceptable; and that the finishing processes of the woven cloth could also be done in commercial mills. The critical points were that every stage of production had to be done in the islands and that Harris Tweed had to be woven, by hand – strictly by foot, as the looms are treadle-driven – at the weaver's own home.

Parliament has more than once legislated for the Harris Tweed trademark; all that the distinctive Orb stands for – and it is the oldest trademark in Britain – was laid down uncompromisingly in the Harris Tweed Act (1993), which established the Harris Tweed Authority:

Harris Tweed means a tweed which has been hand woven by the islanders at their homes in the Outer Hebrides, finished in the islands of Harris, Lewis, North Uist, Benbecula, South Uist and Barra and their several purtenances (The Outer Hebrides) and made from pure virgin wool dyed and spun in the Outer Hebrides.

Every length of final, finished cloth is inspected at the mill – there are two, one in Stornoway and one in Shawbost, north-west Lewis – and every 50 metres stamped with the Orb mark.

Every garment or accessory marketed as Harris Tweed must bear the mark, be it a tie, jacket, skirt or handbag. If it does not, it is not Harris Tweed. And it pays to be careful: it is by no means unknown for certain shops in Edinburgh and elsewhere to place a handful of prominently marked Harris Tweed purses, for instance, amidst a pile of cheap and near-identical imitations from the dappled moors of the People's Republic of China.

Only members of the Harris Tweed Weavers Association are allowed to produce the fabric – an interesting example of a trade union composed entirely of self-employed people – and a silly bid in the 1970s to transfer all production to Stornoway factories was decisively voted down. Production of Harris Tweed peaked around 1981. Thereafter, and for many years, the market steadily declined.

The veil of charity might be drawn over the floundering ineptitudes of this era – and the calamitous sale of the last Stornoway mill to an English merchant who, with vast stockpiles of Harris Tweed jackets to sell for decades to come, laid off most workers. But in 2007, under the leadership of Brian Wilson – a respected journalist and Labour politician, who had held office under Tony Blair – Harris Tweed Hebrides was established, buying and reviving the old mill at Shawbost.

Harris Tweed Hebrides now accounts for around 90 per cent of Harris Tweed production. The industry now employs more than 130 weavers, most on the west side of Lewis, and exports to over 60 countries.

The industry was saved, and thrives anew.

16

LOCH LOMOND

Loch Lomond is – choosing one's words carefully – the largest expanse of enclosed fresh water in Britain; or, more crudely, its largest lake: twenty-seven and a half square miles in surface area, and twenty-four miles long, with a pleasant scatter of islands in its broad southern base.

The loch beside is a significant – and very beautiful – breach in the Highland Boundary Fault, which stretches broadly from Helensburgh on the Firth of Clyde to Stonehaven on Scotland's east coast.

But, being so near Glasgow, Loch Lomond's shores are clotted at weekends and holidays with a great many casual trippers, especially at the southern and very commercialised end by Balloch and Balmaha. Ben Lomond, lowering over the far quieter waters of the north from its eastern shore, stands 3,193 feet (974 metres) tall. It is Scotland's most southern Munro – a mountain of 3,000 feet or more in height – and surely the most climbed, being an undemanding tramp and, again, so convenient for Glasgow.

Just within living memory, Gaelic was still spoken in many of the lochside hamlets and there was once quite a steamer fleet, ferrying mail and supplies up and across Loch Lomond, as well as, in season, many visitors.

The very last, Maid of the Loch – constructed as recently as 1953 and the last paddle steamer ever built in Britain – arrived when tens of thousands still surged to Loch Lomond and the Clyde resorts on their holidays. Accordingly, she was the largest steamer ever built for Lomond cruising; indeed, trade was such that two much older vessels backed her up in the early seasons.

She had to be prefabricated in a Partick yard and brought by road and rail to the loch in sections; hitherto, steamers for Loch Lomond service had been floated up the River Leven, from Dumbarton to Balloch, when in spring spate. (It is said that these half-built ships used to be filled with willing children, so as to squeeze the more easily under the bridges.)

However, as customs changed and the summer hordes vanished, she would prove too big and uneconomic. Withdrawn in 1981, and after long neglect, the Maid of the Loch can now be enjoyed as a static attraction at Balloch Pier, and may yet sail again.

There is strong evidence that Loch Lomond was once a sea loch. Its waters are only 20 feet above sea level, it comes tantalisingly close to Loch Long and the Firth of Clyde at the Arrochar isthmus, and before the First World War there were serious plans – egged on by the Royal Navy – to incorporate Loch Lomond into a massive new ship-canal, whereby their Dreadnoughts could easily traverse the country from the Forth to the Clyde. The scheme, which would have been fabulously expensive and cut some enormous cliffs through Stirlingshire, happily came to nothing.

'The Bonnie Banks o' Loch Lomond'
By yon bonnie banks and by yon bonnie braes,
Where the sun shines bright on Loch Lomond,
Where me and my true love were ever wont to gae,
In the bonnie, bonnie banks of Loch Lomond.

(Chorus)
O ye'll take the high road, and I'll take the low road,
And I'll be in Scotland afore ye,
Where me and my true love will never meet again,
On the bonnie, bonnie banks of Loch Lomond.

There are more than 30 islands dotting the surface, several of which are still inhabited. The largest, Inchmurrin, boasts a ruined castle, once the seat of the Earls of Lennox (Lennox, by the way, being the old name for Dunbartonshire). The islands east of Inchmurrin, towards Balmaha, have long been a nature reserve, thickly wooded in oak and a beloved sanctuary for winter waterfowl. The shores of Loch Lomond generally are well forested with lovely deciduous trees – beech, chestnut, larch, birch, oak – and the bluebell wood just north of Luss, a perfect picture in May, is just one reason why many consider the hamlet the prettiest village in Scotland. Celebrities have come to be married in Luss Parish Church; the community was besides the location for a long-running Scottish Television soap-opera, *Take the High Road*. Properties here fetch vertiginous prices, for no more are allowed to be built.

Ben Lomond is best approached by passenger ferry from the Inverbeg Hotel, at Glen Douglas, to little Rowardennan on the loch's eastern shore (which is otherwise innocent of road). It's an easy climb and the summit, many assert, offers the best vantage point in all Scotland, Ben Lomond being visible even from the suburban hills of Edinburgh. It allows 'unusually wide views far across the Lowland Plain to Tinto Hill in Lanarkshire', murmurs W.H. Murray, 'to Stirling and the Forth estuary, and south-west across the many arms of the Firth of Clyde to the Arran hills, to Kintyre and Jura, even to the Atlantic beyond. Close below, Loch Lomond gleams placidly, silver-grey, or blue, or black as gun-metal'.

Inversnaid is linked by road to Loch Katrine and its venerable wee steamer, the Sir Walter Scott, built in 1899 and still going strong. This is MacGregor country, and 'Rob Roy's Cave' – one suspects he had several such hidey-holes – is by Loch Lomond's lapping waters a little north of Inversnaid. (The selfsame cave, in similar circumstances, had been used by a skulking Robert the Bruce in 1306.) Here, too, Wordsworth – staying at Inversnaid in August 1803 – saw the luckless ferryman's daughter, inspiring him to write an exceptionally bad poem; the village was more fortunate, in 1881, with the eponymous lines of Gerard Manley Hopkins, concluding:

Degged with dew, dappled with dew
Are the groins of the braes that the brook treads
  through,
Wiry heathpacks, flitches of fern,
And the beadbonny ash that sits over the burn.
What would the world be, once bereft
Of wet and of wildness? Let them be left, O let them
  be left, wildness and wet,
Long live the weeds and the wilderness yet.

Far more famed than his 'Inversnaid', though – arguably, still more than the loch itself – is 'The Bonnie Banks o' Loch Lomond', doubtless the world's best-known Scottish song after 'Auld Lang Syne'. It's a traditional folk song, though we do not know who wrote it. It did not appear in print until 1841, and there are various versions of the lyrics and two distinct (though evidently related) airs. Most theories see it as the tale of a Jacobite prisoner – or, more accurately, two Jacobite prisoners (brothers? buddies?) captured in the terrible weeks after Culloden, one capriciously to be executed, the other no less capriciously released, as Hanoverian forces were prone to do for sport. The song has been covered by innumerable artists, perhaps most popularly by the Gaelic folk-rock group, Runrig, and most perfectly, perhaps, by Alistair Ogilvy, a talented young singer from Strathblane.

DID YOU KNOW?

....

The Loch Lomond & The Trossachs National Park has been welcoming masses of visitors since 19 July 2002. The park was officially opened by HRH the Princess Royal the following week.

....

Ben Lomond, a 974-metre mountain within Loch Lomond & The Trossachs National Park, is a popular choice for walkers and mountaineers alike. Over 30,000 people make it to the top of the mountain each year, and are rewarded with fantastic views of the full length of Loch Lomond.

....

The Highland Boundary Fault, which geologically divides the Highlands from the Lowlands, runs in a south-westerly direction through the islands of Inchcailloch, Torrinch, Creinch and Inchmurrin, which sit on Loch Lomond.

....

17

HIGHLAND CATTLE

The Highland cow, a great shaggy thing of vast horns and gentle mien (though formidably hardy), is perhaps the most iconic Scottish beast of all.

Artists since Landseer have churned out works, from the grand to the icky, of the shaggy, noble cattle a-paddle in lochs as the mist weeps in rugged Scottish hills.

Hotels in Germany have bought Highlanders simply for their ornamental charm. They've been used to sell a famous brand of Scottish toffee. And with their stocky leg-at-each-corner build and that distinctive fringe obscuring their eyes, they embody to great degree our tough, enigmatic national character.

While the 'breed standard' has been about since Victorian times and written records go back into the 1700s, Highland cattle have been around for a very long time. (Confusingly, they were traditionally described as 'black cattle' which, these days, they rarely are.)

'Of all the representatives of our British bovine breeds,' pants the 1885 author of the Highland Cattle Herd Book, 'the Highlander has the grandest and most picturesque head; it is, indeed, to his head that he owes his great favour among artists. As a rule, it is most proportionate to the body of the animal, and is broad between the eyes, while short from the eyes to the point of the muzzle. The forelock between the eyes should be wide, long and bushy, and any nakedness or bareness there is certain to detract from the appearance of the animal …

'The eyes should be bright and full, and denoting, when excited, high courage. When viewed sideways, there should be a proportionate breadth of the jawbones readily observable, when compared with the width of the head in front, whilst the muzzle should, when looked at from a similar point, be short, though very broad in front, and with the nostrils fully distended, and indicating breeding in every way. One of the most noteworthy features in a Highlander is, of course, the horns …

'The hair, of which there should be a great profusion, more particularly on the parts indicated, should be long and gracefully waved, very much as in what dog-breeders denote wavy-coated retrievers. To have a curl is to possess a decided fault, and one which has of late years become unfortunately too common in some folds … The usual colours are black, brindled, red, yellow, and dun, and there is considerable difference of opinion among breeders as to which is preferable.'

'Folds' of Highland cattle – enthusiasts refuse to speak of herds – can be found all over Europe, on the Faroe Islands and even in odd corners of England. But it is on the braes of the Highlands and the crofts of the Hebrides where they truly belong and where they happily thrive in conditions no other breed of cow would tolerate.

This is an exceptionally tough and hardy animal. Their magnificent coats afford full protection from gnawing Scottish winds and driving Scottish rain. They prosper even on the mean forage and scant grasses of our Highland moor, their unique physiology converting such indifferent fare to magnificent, buttery beef. They are extraordinarily skilled in nosing out food even in the most challenging mountain environment and will chomp all sorts of things softer cows would disdain.

Highlanders are so robust they need no winter housing and routinely (and seldom with difficulty) calve outdoors. They are also exceptionally long-lived – many Highland cows are still breeding at 18 or more – and, by the way, they are wonderful mums.

It is no surprise that, in recent decades, they have been exported to like and challenging environments far round the world and that, today, Highlanders contentedly chew the cud 10,000 feet high in the Andes. They are often cross-bred – typically, a Highland cow is served by a Shorthorn bull – to make hardy, mass-market hill-cattle, with especially good meat on a more commercially profitable carcass. Highland-Shorthorn cross cows are prized as 'sucklers', inheriting all the motherliness of their rugged mothers; crossed themselves with, say, a Charolais or Limousin bull, they are today central to Scotland's lucrative beef industry.

They are a beef breed and 'Guaranteed Pure Highland Beef' is superlative, sells at a premium and has to be hunted down at the best butchers. Customers particularly prize it as, in an age of factory farming and overdosed, overmedicated, pellet-fed grub, they know that Highland beef is from free-range and naturally reared animals – lean, beautifully marbled meat with less fat and cholesterol, and more protein and iron, than any other and of distinctive succulence and flavour.

Though the horns might suggest otherwise, Highlanders are exceptionally gentle animals of a most docile disposition and, indeed, are apt to be shy around people. Any cow, though, can turn very angry indeed, if she senses the least threat to her calf, and this should be remembered and respected.

Their majesty apart, it is their ability to thrive, with little attention, on terrain that would feed little else – and to profit – that has for long made them vital in the human economy of the Highlands. But for these magnificent animals, in great tracts of the north and west, there would be no people today.

DID YOU KNOW?

Records show that the Highland cow is the oldest registered breed in the world. Their 'herd book', which records the pedigree of cattle, predates all others by far.

Despite their appearance, Highland cattle aren't actually that large in comparison to other breeds. On average, bulls weigh approximately 800kg and cows can reach up to 500kg.

Today, the Highland cow is viewed primarily as a beef cow. In recent years, it has gained popularity in many western countries due to its low cholesterol levels.

Highland cows are perfectly adapted to harsh conditions they live in. Their thick undercoats keep them warm, long eyelashes protect their eyes from rain and biting winds and they use their horns to rake away snow to get to food.

18

ROBERT BURNS

'Robert Burns has something for everyone,' mused James McMillan in 1969. 'He is all the faces of Scotland, except those the Scots are loath to show the world.

'He is sentimental and sardonic and drunken and repentant and home-loving and wench-wooing and idealistic and sceptical. And he is always patriotic. There is nothing mean or thrawn, sullen, sour or dour about Burns. He mocks those features in the Scots character, and the Scots who unite to honour him want to mock them too. For they know they suffer from them.'

Robert Burns was born in Alloway, Ayrshire, on 25 January 1759; and died in Dumfries on 21 July 1796. He was only thirty-seven years old and had never, really, been allowed to be young: ill-nourished, put too young to the plough, he was broken in adolescence by physical toil beyond modern imagining. As an adult he was never strong and in his final years, for all his creativity and song-collecting expeditions, he was what we would now regard as a career civil servant, more of an Establishment figure than he cared to affect or his millions of abiding admirers care to acknowledge. He was, besides, an active and ardent Freemason, an important factor in his rapid, posthumous deification.

Too much was made – even in his own lifetime – of Burns as an untutored native genius; a 'heaven-

taught ploughman poet'. He himself rather played up to it. Certainly he had not received much formal, structured education. But his teacher, John Murdoch – engaged when the boy was seven and who taught him and several other local sprogs for an intense three years – had quickly grasped his abilities and given young Burns the tools to school himself. As James A. Mackay points out in his biography of the Bard, he

was a voracious reader who knew his Bible, the plays of Shakespeare and Vanbrugh, the poetry of Milton, Dryden and Pope, and the novels of his own time. He was fluent in French and knew as much Latin as most educated men of his time. He had studied mathematics (a prerequisite of his excise calling) and took a keen interest in the social and political questions of the period. His voluminous correspondence with men and women of all degrees in society reveals a man of high intelligence, candour and independent mind.

Only William Shakespeare occupies more paragraphs in the Oxford Dictionary of Quotations. No poet, anywhere, has been more widely translated – into

Re-opened in 2009 following extensive restoration work, this small, circular 'temple' to Burns is in the Neo-Greek style typical of Georgian era Edinburgh and is situated on Regent Road at the southerly foot of Calton Hill looking out to Arthur's seat in Holyrood Park.

fifty languages and counting – and none enjoys greater international appeal or transcends more boundaries of culture, faith and thought. Certainly no poet has had more statues erected in his honour (180 at the most recent count). And the last Russian edition of his works sold more than a million copies.

'He knew the nature of man and woman opposed to the bare elements of existence,' argues author James Barke in his introduction in Poems and Songs of Robert Burns. 'His experience, if searing, was fundamental and therefore universal. It is this supreme quality that makes Burns the first world-poet. Burns embraces all humanity. Humanity has, in turn, embraced him … The unco guid, the rigidly righteous, the Holy Willies, the Hornbooks, the Cotters, the Man made to Mourn, the Mouse – none of these is exclusive to eighteenth-century Ayrshire. They are universal and timeless.'

It's all the odder because Burns wrote almost all his verses in Scots – a dialect of English hard for most to follow without a glossary; he also wrote a very great deal of it (a typical edition of the complete works runs to over 700 pages in very small print); and much of it is slight. Some of it is, besides, downright filthy.

But, at his best, Burns is adored in China, cherished in Russia – at the height of the Cold War, ponderous Soviet visitors rated a pilgrimage to the birthplace of the author of 'A Man's A Man For A' That' almost as highly as the obligatory pad to Karl Marx's grave in the Highgate cemetery – and quoted in the United States for those elements that give his finest verses abiding power.

For one, Burns is tremendous fun: 'Tam O'Shanter', his last great work, is a mock-heroic romp thinly disguised as an Awful Moral Warning – but Tam gets away with it, doesn't he? And, for another, Burns is capable of great tenderness, seeing nobility in the prosaic and pathos in the commonplace.

There is besides a sustained theme – or at least an undercurrent – through Robert Burns's poems, that of support for the underdog and the outsider. It can be exaggerated; he also wrote some bilious, jingoistic verse in praise of Britain and King George, and undoubtedly trimmed to attain – and hold – his lucrative excise office. He was happy to swear a long and ponderous oath to the Sovereign in 1789 and a colleague praised him as an 'active, faithful and zealous officer' who 'gives the most unremitting attention to his duties'. A man had, after all, to get by.

All his best work, though, was underpinned by extraordinary powers of observation – an ear for the rhythms of speech, and the turn and cadence of a melody; an astute knowledge of human nature – though not, fundamentally, of human wickedness.

Though there is, of course, a dark side.

Even by the standards of male behaviour at the time, Burns was both incontinent and callous, as journalist George Rosie grimly related in 2000:

Modern Scotland likes to chortle over the notion of the Bard as a roguish lad with an eye for a pretty woman. But there is more to it than that. By rights, he should rank high in the demonology of left-inclined feminists. All the evidence is that Burns was a selfish and reckless womaniser who had no compunction about abandoning the young women he impregnated. He fathered 13 children by six different women ... His

Sir Walter Scott never forgot meeting Burns as a child. He described his person as 'strong and robust; his manners rustic, not clownish, a sort of dignified plainness and simplicity which received part of its effect perhaps from knowledge of his extra-ordinary talents. His features are presented in Mr Nasmyth's picture but to me it conveys the idea that they are diminished, as if seen in perspective. I think his countenance was more massive than it looks in any of the portraits ... there was a strong expression of shrewdness in all his lineaments; the eye alone, I think, indicated the poetical character and temperament. It was large, and of a dark cast, and literally glowed when he spoke with feeling or interest. I never saw such another eye in a human head, though I have seen the most distinguished men of my time.'

attitude to them all was dreadful. The fact is, Burns's sexual strategy was **** and dump: to leave the girls with fatherless children and then sneer at their only source of support – the Kirk.

What cannot be doubted is his appetite for extraordinarily hard work – churning out poems and letters, and frequent song-hunting excursions, all the while attending to the duties of his office and running the latest bleak farm. And, in short order, it killed him; Robert Burns finally succumbed to a heart infection, probably the result of a tooth-extraction in his last winter.

It was his brothers in Freemasonry who first began annually to commemorate the poet's birth with a 'Burns Supper' – more recognisable to Scots then than now as a calculated parody of the Scottish Communion service – and it is this, more than anything else, which fast established there-was-a-lad-that-came-from-Kyle as less of a reputation than a cult. The phenomenon has long been global, and reflects a curious elasticity to all that Burns was and represents.

19

LOCH NESS

Loch Ness is by far the biggest of the three freshwater lochs along the Great Glen boundary fault; indeed, with a surface area of 21.8 square miles and a depth of 812 feet at Nessie's Lair, its volume is greater than that of all the lakes of England and Wales put together. But the water is dark, peaty stuff and underwater visibility is dire ...

Even with the brightest submersible lights, visibility is scarcely 30 feet. And that matters a great deal when – of course – Loch Ness is far less famous in itself than for what millions the world over think is living in it.

Culturally, the Loch Ness Monster is a most modern phenomenon. With one very ambivalent exception, there wasn't a single sighting or tale of Nessie recorded until 22 July 1933, when Mr and Mrs George Spicer saw 'a most extraordinary form of creature' crossing the road in front of them as they motored down the loch, mid-afternoon. It was of a loathsome-looking greyish colour, like a dirty elephant or a rhinoceros. It had a very long and thin neck, which

undulated up and down, and was contorted into a series of half hoops. The body was much thicker, and moved across the road in a series of jerks. The whole looked like a huge snail with a long neck …

By the time they pulled up and jumped out, the beast had disappeared. Still, there followed a glut of Nessie sightings – many, curiously, of a creature lumbering about on land, not in the water. And why all this activity (or mass-hallucination)? That same year, 1933, the modern A82 had just been completed along the loch's northern shore, bringing a great many of the 'motor-tourists' to these parts.

Hitherto, the monster had never before been seen or heard of. Believers can brandish just one averred historic account, the confrontation of a 'ferocious monster' by St Columba himself, in the seventh century AD who (according to his cooing biographer Adomnán) saw off the beast with a single command and a wave of his stick.

But there are self-evident inconveniences. For one, it happened in the River Ness, not the loch, and in any event the story may have a simpler explanation – it could easily have been a cross bull-seal or even a walrus. So the sudden rise of Nessie, well within living memory, should make us rather sceptical.

The other great problem is that most modern reports and blurry images are of something remarkably similar – a huge, long-tailed hump-backed reptile which, fans argue, is a plesiosaur, somehow still enduring in the Loch Ness ecosystem.

But a dinosaur of any sort is still, unambiguously, a reptile, and if there is one thing a reptile cannot abide it is cold. The average temperature of Loch Ness is only 5.5 degrees Centigrade – in which no reptile could survive; the hypothesis of a warm-blooded monster then calls for both a mighty food supply (which there isn't) and the repeated need to surface to breathe.

In any event, the plesiosaur theory was blown apart in 2006 by Cambridge boffin Leslie Noè who – with a fossilised skeleton to hand – showed that the osteology of the neck would make it quite impossible for one to raise its head, swan-like, out of the water … as most Nessie believers insist she does.

Still dafter is the theory of some sort of subterranean tunnel between Loch Ness and the sea: the loch's surface is 50 feet above sea level and it would simply drain out like a bath.

There are other complications. Perspective can be easily distorted when looking over expanses of water: small objects near to hand – waterfowl, otters and so on – can be thought great beasties far away. And the loch is especially prone to 'seiches' – surface waves which often run against the wind, making any drifting object look as if it were actively swimming.

And there has been untold cheating. The celebrated 'Surgeon's Photograph' of the monster, avowedly taken by Colonel Robert Wilson in 1934, was unmasked 60 years later as a fake. A 'big-game hunter' claimed to have found monster footprints in the ground; these were fast proven to have been made with a stuffed, dried hippo's foot. A chunk of fossilised plesiosaur, found at the lochside in 2003, was found not to be of local rock – and so had been deliberately planted there.

The general atmosphere of hysteria is evident as you drive through Drumnadrochit; practically side-by-side, in glowering rivalry, two vast ex-hotels now proclaim themselves respectively as the 'Original Loch Ness Monster Exhibition' and the 'Official Loch Ness Monster Exhibition'.

And yet … If Nessie does not exist, one would very much like her to.

20

PS *WAVERLEY*

The famed PS *Waverley*, launched at Partick, Glasgow, in 1946, has been for the past 40 years or so the last seagoing paddle steamer in the world.

She has been run during this time on a non-profit basis by the Paddle Steamer Preservation Society, to whom she was sold in 1974 for just £1. So began her a second career as one of the country's best-loved tourist attractions.

Though built, post-war, for limited operations on the upper Firth of Clyde, with compensation funds from the government after her 1899 namesake was sunk, on active service, at Dunkirk, the *Waverley* now spends spells each year sailing in the West Highlands, the Bristol Channel and the Thames estuary.

She has twice circumnavigated Britain, visited Northern Ireland, the Isle of Man and the coast of France, and a decade ago was extensively refurbished and rebuilt – an exercise that deftly incorporated modern safety features within her meticulous 1940s decoration and furnishing – thus securing her operation for decades to come.

And she has, accordingly, long been a national institution, supported along the way by a kindly press and a reputation for being deliciously accident-prone: few Clyde seasons pass without the odd bump and scrape.

The *Waverley* is not just the last pleasure-steamer in service; she's a living monument to the innovation and engineering that made the Clyde the workshop of the world and which, at the peak of Empire, built and launched a quarter – annually – of the earth's new ships.

It was James Watt, a native of Greenock, who devised the world's first efficient steam engine, while on Glasgow's Forth and Clyde Canal in 1803, with his steam-powered *Charlotte Dundas*, William Symington proved the new technology was practical for ships. It was Henry Bell of Helensburgh, though, in 1812, who launched the first successful passenger steamboat service in Europe, with the little paddler, *Comet*, built to his instructions by a firm in Port Glasgow and offering regular runs from Glasgow to Greenock.

Bell was fast eclipsed by other, shrewder operators, but it was not just steamship travel that he had invented — it was the wholly new concept of a reliable timetable. The Clyde soon became a major centre of ship construction, aided by a recent deepening of the river, Glasgow's venture-capitalist culture, its ample local resources of coal and iron, and every variety of skilled tradesman — riveters, platers, frame-benders, carpenters, boiler-makers, ropeworkers, chain-makers …

It was the Great War, in all its horror and economic consequence, that turned the tide against this; the late 1950s and the rapid expansion of private car ownership began (swiftly) to put Clyde cruising out of fashion.

When she entered service in 1947 and in the colours of the London and North-Eastern Railway, the *Waverley* was based at Craigendoran, voyaging largely up Loch Long, just one of two dozen sturdy steamers on the Firth. With railway nationalisation the following year, she was consigned to the drab buff funnels of state ownership; over the years she saw more extensive use as motor vessels and the first generation of car ferries slowly whittled her elegant sisters away.

By 1969, the *Waverley* was one of just six surviving steamers in Scottish west-coast service and at the end of 1973 Caledonian MacBrayne saw no option but to withdraw her. In an imaginative gesture, though, she was offered as a gift — the nominal £1 was simply to make the transaction legal — and the young, tweedy local enthusiasts took on responsibility for the steamer.

Caledonian MacBrayne no doubt assumed that the paddler would survive merely as a static floating clubhouse. But her new owners had very different ideas, though in 1974, at least, the churn of paddle-wheels was heard nowhere on the Clyde. It took many months of volunteer effort, with scant help from public funds, to see her back in service (in her original funnel colours) for the summer of 1975.

Somehow she was kept going by her new owners and from 1977 she enjoyed brief cruise seasons elsewhere in the British Isles. In 1981, she was hugely rejuvenated by a new boiler. A rebuild in 2003–04 greatly improved her appearance and accommodation, and, though the high price of fuel-oil has been a recent strain, she washes gloriously on.

The *Waverley* usually begins her summer with a programme of West Highland cruising. By late June she's on her Clyde schedule — based at Ayr early in the week and Glasgow from Friday and through the weekend; late August sees her in the Bristol Channel and she ends, in autumn, with some Thames cruising and a final Clyde run or two. Volunteers tend to her paintwork and so on during the winter Glasgow lay-up and she is normally dry-docked and overhauled in late May.

For her size – the ship has a gross tonnage of 693 and is but 240 feet long – the *Waverley* can hold a considerable crowd in remarkable comfort and is certificated for up to 860 passengers in British coastal waters. On the promenade deck she boasts an elegant observation lounge and, aft, a pleasant saloon with light refreshments available and a selection of the day's newspapers.

On the main deck below, there is a large bar forward, and a spacious dining saloon, with another snug – the Clyde Bar – immediately below this. The great attraction on her main deck, though, are her mighty engines, fully open to public view; a joyous vision of pistons and cylinders, eccentrics and connecting-rods in a symphony of brass and gun-metal. Passengers of all ages can spend an age leaning at the rail, hypnotised by the thrust and surge of this splendid technology, intoxicated by the scent of steam and hot oil …

Contrary to widespread belief, the two paddle-wheels cannot be operated independently. The old girl, though, is surprisingly manoeuvrable and – in an emergency – can be brought to a halt from top speed (her normal, in service, is fifteen to sixteen knots) in just over her own length. That would, however, be excessively exciting for passengers.

DID YOU KNOW?

PS *Waverley* was built on the Clyde, and was named after Sir Walter Scott's first novel.

In 1974, at the end of PS *Waverley*'s working life, she was famously bought for £1 by the Paddle Steamer Preservation Society. She was the world's last sea-going paddle steamer.

2003 saw the completion of a huge restoration project, which returned PS *Waverley* to the original 1940s style in which she was built. This was made possible with major grants from the Heritage Lottery Fund and the Paddle Steamer Preservation Society, as well as Glasgow City Council and other local authorities.

Paddle Steamers made an important contribution to the war effort as minesweepers in both World Wars.

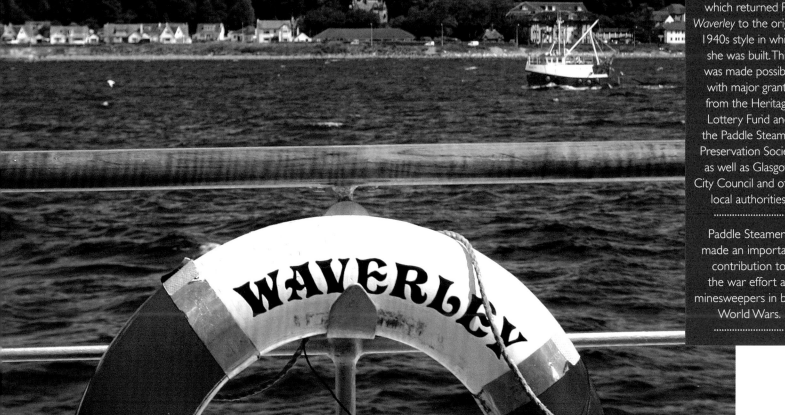

21

WILLIAM McGONAGALL

If Robert Burns is one of the greatest poets ever to walk this planet, William Topaz McGonagall was assuredly one of the worst writers in verse in the English language.

In fact, he is so bad he is hilarious – all the funnier because, humourless to the last, tin-eared and ponderous, he never had the remotest idea of just how awful his poems were. And in a perverse triumph, his entire *oeuvre* is in print to this day.

Though born in Edinburgh in 1825, of Irish parentage, McGonagall – whose day-job was as a handloom-weaver – spent almost all his life in Dundee and is indelibly associated with that city, not least because of his most infamous composition, 'The Tay Bridge Disaster':

Beautiful Railway Bridge of the Silv'ry Tay! Alas! I am very sorry to say
That ninety lives have been taken away
On the last Sabbath day of 1879,
Which will be remember'd for a very long time …

And so on, through eight relentless verses, beating you about the brain like a sock-load of wet sand, concluding:

It must have been an awful sight, To witness in the dusky moonlight,

While the Storm Fiend did laugh, and angry did bray,
*   Along the Railway Bridge of the Silv'ry Tay,*
Oh! ill-fated Bridge of the Silv'ry Tay, I must now
*   conclude my lay*
By telling the world fearlessly without the least
*   dismay, That your central girders would not have*
*   given way,*
At least many sensible men do say,

Had they been supported on each side with
*   buttresses, At least many sensible men confesses,*
For the stronger we our houses do build, The less
*   chance we have of being killed.*

McGonagall was evidently good at his day-job – for only the most skilled handloom craftsmen survived at a time of rapid mechanisation – and domestically happy; in 1846, he married Jean King, and in time they enjoyed five sons and two daughters. The first sign of his capacity for self-delusion was a brief attempt at acting. He had to pay for the privilege of the starring role in a local performance of Macbeth – at the end of which he refused to die, convinced the actor playing MacDuff was trying to upstage him. Then, as he notes in his turgid memoirs, 'The most startling incident in my life was the time I discovered myself to be a poet, which was in the year 1877 …'

His very first poem was 'An Address to the Rev. George Gilfillan', an eccentric local preacher of most limited ability, whose response to the clunking lines was at least accurate: 'Shakespeare never wrote anything like this.' Encouraged and inflated, McGonagall then made determined bids to win the patronage of Queen Victoria: in July 1878, he walked all the way to Balmoral, only to be denied admission; in 1880, he tried to establish himself in London, and in 1887, still more heroically, in New York. Both ventures were equally unsuccessful.

McGonagall supported himself as best he could by reciting his verse in local halls and public houses, selling sheets of it in the street, and for a time made fifteen shillings a night declaiming it in a local circus – before the crowd were positively encouraged to pelt him with stuff. It appears he did not mind this in the slightest, but the turn soon became so raucous that

the city magistrates simply banned his performances, to the poet's wounded chagrin:

Fellow citizens of Bonnie Dundee
Are ye aware how the magistrates have treated me?
  Nay, do not stare or make a fuss
When I tell ye they have boycotted me from
  appearing in Royal Circus,
Which in my opinion is a great shame, And a
  dishonour to the city's name …

By 1890, McGonagall was in dire financial straits and began threatening to leave Dundee. (Someone quipped that he would likely have stayed a little longer had he realised the city's name rhymed with 1893.) Friends did raise subscriptions to publish a collection of his verses, *Poetic Gems*, however. Finally, in 1894, he repaired to Perth and, the following year, to Edinburgh. It was about this time he fell for what was really rather a cruel hoax – an averred letter from representatives of King Thibaw Min of Burma, announcing McGonagall now enjoyed the grace and style of 'Sir Topaz McGonagall, Grand Knight of the Holy Order of the White Elephant Burma'. Yet the poet joyously advertised himself in these terms for the rest of his life (and went to his grave blithely innocent of the truth).

In 1895, he returned to Edinburgh. Initial success – or at least attention – did not last long and by 1900, old and frail, he was wholly dependent on the charity of those about him. He died in 1902 and is buried in a pauper's grave in Greyfriars Kirkyard; only in 1999 was a tablet erected in his memory:

McGonagall
Poet and Tragedian
'I am your gracious Majesty ever faithful to Thee,

William McGonagall, the Poor Poet, That lives in
Dundee.'

It is probable that McGonagall suffered from Asperger's, or a similar autistic-spectrum disorder, and was unable to sense that folk were laughing at *him* rather than *with him*; this was reinforced in his delusional world by paranoid defence mechanisms. Certainly he seems not to have comprehended the general, joyous derision of his work. And yet he gloriously resists oblivion.

To be sure, 'his audiences threw rotten fish at him', muses Chris Hunt, who runs the McGonagall Online website in his honour, 'the authorities banned his performances, and he died a pauper over a century ago. But his books remain in print to this day, and he's remembered and quoted long after more talented contemporaries have been forgotten.'

22

GOLF

This infuriating, highly addictive sport
is a Scottish invention. And it is, indeed,
both royal and ancient.

We read of it in Edinburgh as early as 1457 … and it seems to have been played rather too much. For in that same year, the Scottish Parliament passed an Act at the behest of King James II, who wanted to suppress – or at least discourage – the game. Fit young men should be practising their archery.

The first known female golfer was Mary, Queen of Scots. In March 1567, on holiday at Seton in East Lothian, she enjoyed a round on Musselburgh Links course. It was disastrous timing, for only a few days earlier her ghastly young husband Henry, Lord Darnley, had been murdered: the public were appalled. The merry widow did not much longer enjoy her throne.

While similar games with sticks, wee balls and holes in the ground are recorded in Roman times, there is little doubt that the sport as we know it today began in Scotland. Evidence suggests that in 1552 a charter allowed the people of St Andrews to play golf on the Links, making the Old Course in the town the oldest golf course in the world.

It's a deceptively simple activity – trying to whack your little ball around a nine- or 18-hole course with as few whacks as possible – and unusual among ball games in that there is no requirement for a standardised playing area. A typical golf course is a micromanaged park with close-shaved greens, some natural hazards (trees, dunes, ponds and streams) and some mischievously engineered ones, such as the sandy bunker. You need a variety of clubs for different drives, shots, chips and putts; and a self-consciously grand golfer will have a lad or 'caddie' to carry them around in his train. (That's a great Scots word, born of the French 'cadet'; the 'caddies' were originally a sort of Edinburgh vigilante-force and professional street guides, with their own dark code of honour, textbook knowledge of the city and an acute grasp of local gossip.) One occasionally hears of the 'nineteenth hole'. This is not, in fact, a hole but the golf club's bar for post-match refreshment.

A 'hole in one' – sinking your ball in a single stroke from the starting tee – is every golfer's lifetime ambition. A hazard of the feat, though, is that you must afterwards stand everyone a drink at the nineteenth hole.

In golf, as a standard game has 18 holes of play, the nineteenth hole is a slang term for a pub, bar, or restaurant on or near the golf course, very often the clubhouse itself.

The rules of golf are elaborate, often officious, and administered by the sort of tough old men who have faces like sides of beef. Since 2004 it's been in the hands of a hands-across-the-sea body called the R&A, a joint venture between the world's oldest golf club – the Royal and Ancient Golf Club of St Andrews in Fife, begotten in 1754 – and the less picturesquely styled United States Golf Association.

The first commandment can be found on the back cover of most rule books and is simply: 'Play the ball as it lies, play the course as you find it, and if you cannot do either, do what is fair.' But the self-appointed gods of golf have not been above banning , for instance, new designs of ball or club that make the game a little easier, notably one ingenious golf club that allegedly eliminated 'the dribbles' – an affliction so terrible that golfers never talk of it, lest they get it.

The Royal and Ancient Golf Club is notoriously grand. It also, till September 2014, refused to admit women to its membership. Though no longer with global power over the game, the international embarrassment became too much. It still hosts in turn perhaps its most hallowed championship, the Open – as do other Scottish clubs: Muirfield in East Lothian, and Troon in Ayrshire.

Muirfield, in fact, is so haughty that attaining membership is said to be one of three essential marks of true social arrival in Edinburgh. (The others being membership of the New Club – a wood-panelled hive of crashing bores behind a ghastly concrete façade on the capital's Princes Street – and of the Royal Company of Archers, the Queen's official bodyguard when she resides each summer in the city.)

Notwithstanding, golf remains an exceptionally democratic and accessible sport in Scotland. Many towns have public links and major cities boast courses run by the local authority. (One beauty, on the craggy flanks of the Braid Hills in Edinburgh, runs cheek-by-jowl with the greens and hazards of the frightfully posh Mortonhall Golf Club course, players eyeing each other suspiciously over a stern stone wall.)

By contrast, to great degree in England and emphatically so in the United States and elsewhere, the game is very much one for the rich. It is whispered, cynically, that many take it up simply to get on in business. Even that some take it up purely to get away from their wives.

For those otherwise immune to golf's maddening charms, it remains – in words generally attributed to Mark Twain – a good walk spoiled.

23

POLICE

Everyone knows that London is the home of the world's very first modern-style, municipal police force, right? Wrong. That honour goes to the City of Glasgow.

In fact, in a recent humiliation at the hands of the Advertising Standards Authority, London's Metropolitan Police had to promise (in writing) never to make the same claim again.

From the mid-eighteenth century, Glasgow – at the time of the 1745 Rising, still rather a small and pastoral place – grew rapidly, and by 1779 the city's 'baillies' (magistrates) began their first efforts to maintain a force for law and order. It took a decade of fits and starts – the campaign for parliamentary funding would take even longer – but by 1789 the first professional police officers turned out. All eight of them.

Tiny as the force was, and varied as were its duties – they did not just patrol streets, but swept them and fought fires – the elements of what we now regard as true policing were all there. It was under civilian control (there was an official Watch Committee, of elected commissioners); the officers wore uniform, with numbered badges and the label POLICE; and they were recruited with great care for background and character. The role, as was made very clear, was not primarily to catch criminals but to prevent crime – a respected, high-visibility force pacing the city streets.

Glasgow policeman wearing a cap with the chequered 'Sillitoe tartan' band.

Sir Percy Sillitoe.

They only lasted a year; parliament was then a remote body in the south, with general contempt for Scottish interests. But in 1800, the Glasgow Police Act received Royal Assent – nearly three decades before Sir Robert Peel established London's 'bobbies' – and the city has been policed ever since.

It was a two-tier system: a very small force of officers – three sergeants and six constables – and a larger body of sixty-eight plain 'watchmen'. They, armed only with a lantern and a stave, were by shift fixed sentries at given locations; the officers actively patrolled. As an early sign of the hazards of a city which, even then, had a brutal 'blade' culture, the neckbands of their uniforms were reinforced with stiff leather.

From such modest beginnings, the City of Glasgow Constabulary grew and grew. Its bounds waxed, and waxed again, as the city devoured hitherto separate surrounding burghs – Gorbals, Anderston and, in 1912, such fiefs as Govan, Partick and Scotstoun. From 1861, they enjoyed new technology – the electric telegraph – and from 1878 a horse-drawn van for the movement of prisoners. By 1900 the force had 1,355 officers and men; and in 1904 the first detectives were appointed.

In 1931, though, came dramatic change, with the appointment of Percy J. Sillitoe as Chief Constable. Sillitoe was not Glaswegian – he was not even a Scot – but the astute Londoner, full of ideas and initiatives, would prove not just the ideal boss for a force under unprecedented pressures (Glasgow, in the 1930s, was a byword for street-fighting, razor-gangs and local government corruption) but a man of abiding influence on policing the world over.

His immediate concern was visibility. The mighty helmets of London coppers were never sported in Scotland, but the caps of Glasgow's policemen – of whom a high proportion, by the way, were enormous Highlanders – were scarcely distinctive in an age when all sorts of public servants (postmen, milkmen, station-porters and so on) wore them. Sillitoe, inspired by the Glengarry bonnets of Scottish soldiers, decreed that police caps have unique black-and-white diced bands. This 'Sillitoe tartan' stood out a mile and was swiftly adopted by forces throughout Britain and, indeed, overseas.

Another concern was communication. Sillitoe had a network of police telephone-boxes erected throughout the city, not just for officers to summon assistance but to call in regularly during their beat. These were initially painted bright red, though by the 1970s – when they became obsolete – they were blue. A good example survives on Glasgow's Buchanan Street.

The idea was widely copied and, of course, was in 1963 lifted (in a stuck chameleon-circuit joke) for the Tardis – the personal transport of Doctor Who.

Sillitoe also brought in the first wireless-radio communication for police cars – though there were still very few of these. He ruthlessly reorganised, ordering his command into seven major divisions, closing 13 unnecessary police stations. He greatly expanded civilian background and administrative staff, and new departments were set up expressly to process fingerprints and photographs. He fought town-hall graft – in his years of service, five city councillors would be jailed – and waged war, with success, on Glasgow's brutal and arrogant gangs. More daringly still, Sillitoe insisted on mandatory retirement after 30 years of police service. By 1943, when he was transferred to command of the Kent Constabulary, Glasgow had the most modern and professional force in the world.

Sillitoe's career ended both in glory – as Director-General of MI5 – and sour defeat: he retired in 1953, with a knighthood, but under the cloud of the shock 1951 defection to Russia from his department of Guy Burgess and Donald MacLean, who, it emerged, had long been Soviet spies. He had suspected nothing – and never quite lived it down.

In 1975, as a consequence of local government reorganisation, the City of Glasgow Constabulary was subsumed into the new, mighty Strathclyde Police. In 2013, like every other force, it came under the unified control of the Scottish Police Authority.

Glasgow was also the stomping ground of a gritty, celebrated and (sadly) fictional copper, Taggart. The Scottish Television production was launched in 1984, starring Mark McManus as the eponymous, tough and world-weary 'tec.

Remarkably, the show (and even its name) survived McManus's early, alcohol-related death in 1994, though his character was wisely laid to rest with him, the abiding ensemble cast instead being led first by DI Jardine (James MacPherson) and from 2002 DI Matt Burke, played by Alex Norton – on ever lower budgets and ever more erratic scheduling.

Sadly axed in 2012 – by which time Taggart was the longest-running TV crime-caper in the world – the show is best remembered for its supposed catchphrase, 'There's been a murrrderrr!', along with the brilliant scripts and fiendish plots of writer Glenn Chandler and its gritty theme song, 'No Mean City', sung by Maggie Bell.

24

ROBERT LOUIS STEVENSON

'All through my boyhood and youth,' Stevenson wrote, 'I was known and pointed out for the pattern of an idler; and yet I was always busy on my own private end, which was to learn to write. I kept always two books in my pocket, one to read, one to write in …'

Robert Louis Stevenson's health was never good. Born in Edinburgh in November 1850, he died young – and far away – still only 44 years old. At that age, Sir Walter Scott had not even begun the Waverley Novels; we can only wonder what Stevenson might have accomplished as an author, granted length of days.

Yet *Treasure Island* alone would have cemented any author's reputation, with its dramatic power, psychological insight and taut, modern penmanship. Stevenson was also an astute essayist and the father of the short-story form. He was an engaging travel writer and it is his misfortune that, on account of his best-known works, he was so long dismissed as just a 'children's author' – middlebrow talent exemplified in nursery verse or ripping yarns for schoolboys.

Stevenson's father, Thomas, was the scion of a renowned lighthouse-building dynasty, whose brilliantly engineered structures (Bell Rock, Skerryvore, the

Robert Louis Stevenson memorial inside the High Kirk of St Giles in Edinburgh.

Butt of Lewis and many more) stand proud and functioning to this day. And his wife, Isabella, was a gentleman; her father, the Reverend Lewis Balfour, was of Fife landowning background and parish minister of Colinton, south-west of Edinburgh. Critically, both he and his daughter had weak chests, a frailty Robert inherited: all his life he would be vulnerable to infection, never strong and always thin. The little boy was inevitably rather coddled and smothered; not just his parents but also his formidable nurse were anxious about him and rather overprotective.

His happiest memories were not of damp, chill townhouses in Edinburgh's New Town, but of regular holidays in the Colinton manse. In 1867 things brightened when the Stevensons removed from the city to Swanston Cottage, a large and attractive home in the eponymous village at the foot of the Pentland Hills, offering a much healthier environment for their son. (You can still take the 'Fly Walk' through Edinburgh's Braidburn Valley Park by which young Robert often tramped to and from this new family home.)

All his life, though, Stevenson felt a profound disappointment to his family. Though put to Edinburgh University in 1867 to study engineering, he hated it. His parents accepted this graciously enough (Thomas himself was an enthusiastic writer as a youth and had been bullied out of it by his father), but suggested he instead read law to give him some sort of fall-back career if he failed in a life of letters. Much more distressing for them was the collapse of their son's once-earnest Christian faith. 'What a damned curse I am to my parents!' he wrote miserably.

It was later that year that Stevenson began to carve out his own life. He won friends and mentors and made the first of several long visits to the south of France, not least for his health. He qualified for the Bar in 1875 but never practised – life was now incessant travel, bouts of writing and bouts of illness; and it was on another French jaunt in 1876 that he met Fanny Van de Grift Osbourne. She was older, American, with an estranged husband and a troupe of children, but she and Stevenson were soon lovers. In 1880, after assorted Californian adventures, they were able to marry.

Out of all this, amidst his ongoing search for some corner of the world where he could comfortably breathe, came the works. A European stravaig begot *Travels With a Donkey in the Cevennes* (1879). In Bournemouth, he penned *The Strange Case of Dr Jekyll and Mr Hyde* (1886). But it was *Treasure Island, or The Mutiny of the Hispaniola* (1883) that was his first big hit. It is not just an abiding thriller but explores themes of moral ambiguity (notably the character of Long John Silver) which are unusual even today in children's fiction. *Kidnapped*, another 'tale for boys', first serialised in 1886, is at once an adventure and a historical novel, notable for its sympathetic portrayal of Highlanders and indebted to the real-life mystery of the Appin Murder – and as good as anything Stevenson ever wrote.

In another vein entirely – because at that time he was so ill as to be unable to concentrate to the degree necessary to plot a story – is 1885's *A Child's Garden of Verses*, with affecting glimpses into the lonely, ailing life of the little boy Stevenson had been:

When I was sick and lay a-bed,
I had two pillows at my head,
And all my toys beside me lay,
To keep me happy all the day.
And sometimes for an hour or so
I watched my leaden soldiers go,
With different uniforms and drills,

Among the bed-clothes, through the hills;
And sometimes sent my ships in fleets
All up and down among the sheets;
Or brought my trees and houses out,
And planted cities all about.
I was the giant great and still
That sits upon the pillow-hill,
And sees before him, dale and plain,
The pleasant land of counterpane …

In June 1888, the Stevensons sailed from San Francisco in a chartered yacht for a protracted exploration of the South Pacific; it was during this island hopscotch he completed *The Master of Ballantrae* (1889). And then in 1890, he bought a substantial tract of land in Western Samoa, settled there, built a house and estate, and became a keen advocate for its people and their interests. They soon adored him and came up with the nickname 'Tusitala' – 'teller of tales' – for him. There was a last great bout of productivity, and plans for a return trip to Scotland were twice postponed. Then on 3 December 1894, he died very suddenly, and there he is buried.

It has not always been fashionable to admire the ailing Scottish wordsmith. Yet Proust thought him 'equal with the greats' and in 1985 correspondence, Graham Greene confessed, 'I admire some of his poems and a great deal of his prose … I think it was Stevenson's method of describing action without adjectives or adverbs which taught me a good deal.' Italo Calvino praised his 'marvellous lightness'; Jorge Luis Borges made no secret of his debt to Stevenson as a craftsman of fiction. And as the late P.D. James put it crisply in 1994, 'He uses English wonderfully, with imagination, with economy, with elegance. We must read him, really, for the sheer pleasure of the language …'

DID YOU KNOW?

One winter evening Stevenson was watching a snowball fight between students and locals in the quadrangle of Edinburgh University. While craning is neck to get a better view, he slipped and was caught by a Policeman, who believed he was involved. He was arrested and marched straight to the Police station. Not good news for a law student!

Stevenson wrote more than 100 original musical compositions and arrangements, including solos, duets, trios and quartets, which he played on the piano or flageolet. His works include ten songs written to his own poetry.

When submitting *Treasure Island* to the children's periodical Young Folks, Stevenson used the nom-de-plume of Captain George North.

25

SALMON

The Atlantic salmon, *salmo salar*, has been rightly dubbed the 'King of Fish'.

For his beauty, his endurance, and an extraordinary instinct that brings him home to breed, through hundreds of miles of ocean, to his own native stream, en route battering through and over and around a host of hazards. He can jump ten clean feet in the air over a waterfall, overpower formidable currents, wait in languid summer shallows – for weeks and weeks – without eating, until the river floods and he can move. It is one thing to hook a salmon; quite another to land him.

The salmon has long, in Gaelic folklore, been a powerful symbol of wisdom; it is also the object of great sport, and delicious eating. And though not unique to Scotland – it breeds in all nations granted coastline in the north Atlantic, and has been introduced to the Pacific – it is extraordinarily identified with us, largely because it was here that Victorian sportsmen (and their scribes) made their fishing such a desirable accomplishment of the gentleman.

The salmon is an anadromous fish – it is born in fresh water, and must return there to breed; but from puberty it makes for the open sea: it is there, voyaging far to the north and about the Arctic Circle, that he eats most voraciously and gains most weight. He is, though, economic with his energy:

salmon do not swim in the ocean so much as surf its currents, and it is rivers especially favoured by these unseen tides that will boast the most salmon. (By contrast, the absence of such helpful drifts has to date frustrated the introduction of Atlantic salmon in New Zealand.)

His is a lifecycle of many phases – and names. The tiny spawn becomes a wispy wee thing called an alevin. The alevin is soon a fry, and then a parr. And then – turning silver-blue and scaly – it is a smolt, hungry for salt water and the ocean's vast larder. From March, smolts make first for the estuary and, once acclimatised to the salinity, the world's one sea. If he returns to spawn – fully mature, but after only one winter away – he is a grilse, of light build and distinctive spotting; if it be two or more winters, he is a fully accredited salmon. But return he will, because return he must.

In its earliest days an alevin lives off its yolk-sac; once that is absorbed, he starts his hunting career, at first for the tiniest water-shrimps and in time other invertebrates, bugs and careless flies. The smolt, once at sea, will feed on plankton and fry; bigger and bolder, he will feast on shrimp, prawn, sand-eels and herring, squid and octopi – and wax fat. But, on the adult's final return to fresh water, he will eat nothing.

A fresh-run fish is accordingly a tight, lithe thing of gleaming beauty; a 'stale' salmon, up his native water for months (and perhaps awaiting long the rain, and ensuing spate, that will allow him at last to reach the 'redds', or spawning-beds of gravel in tiny upper streams) is dark, flabby and a bit of an old kipper. Once spawning is done – the hen sowing her eggs, the cock misting with milt – they are kelts, and then the dreadful journey back to the ocean begins for what are now pretty wretched fish. (Occasionally, by some mishap, a salmon does not mate at all, and if he makes it to the spring he is called a 'baggot' – or unspawned, overwintered salmon.)

Only one in ten salmon – perhaps as few as one in 30 – survives the trip back to the briny; but such will rapidly fatten and recover and, in time, return once more. Examination of a salmon's scales – which record its life rather like the rings of a tree – reveals much: a salmon caught in Loch Maree, one 1933 writer noted, was 13 years old and had spawned four times.

Broadly, there are two sorts of salmon-fishing in Scotland: the great rivers of the east, such as the Tweed, the Tay, the Spey and the Helmsdale, which are broad and shallow, and generally fished from the shore or by wading; and the short 'spate-systems' of the west, where rivers tend to be brief and bring the salmon fast inland (granted summer rains) to one or more freshwater lochs. The rivers of the east are noted for large 'springers', arriving from the North Sea from February onwards; West Highland waters are for rather more abundant (but smaller) summer salmon. It is rare for a fish caught by rod on Lewis to exceed five or six pounds, though far bigger ones are about – a dead salmon, found on a beach by Tong, Lewis, in October 2010, was almost four feet long and weighed 33 lb 4 oz.

Salmon-angling is big business. A length, or 'beat', of the River Spey, at peak season, can be let for tens of thousands of pounds a week; and private angling interests (largely, of course, landlords) have lobbied for decades for tougher conservation measures and ferocious new laws against poaching – notably the Salmon Act 1986. Most estates now insist on catch-and-release and the few that do not invariably have bag-limits. Most of the once-lucrative coastal netting stations have been bought out and closed down, and it is otherwise illegal to catch a salmon by any means at sea, or to sell a salmon caught on the rod.

Yet little has availed to reverse this noble fish's decline. Pollution, from the Industrial Revolution onwards, has done much harm. An exploding seal population, the factory fishing of species on which the adult salmon feeds, and commercial poaching and river mismanagement have also played a part. Many blame modern salmon-farming for damage in estuaries and sea-lochs, though this is disputed: the big problem remains the ruthless netting, in the open sea, by certain fleets from certain countries – Ireland and the Faroes being most widely blamed.

DID YOU KNOW?

The salmon is an important creature in Celtic mythology and poetry, and is often associated them with wisdom and venerability.

Over 50 countries worldwide imported fresh Scottish salmon in 2016.

Typically, salmon are 'anadromous', meaning they hatch in fresh water, migrate to the ocean, then return to fresh water to reproduce. The journey made by those surviving salmon is one of nature's greatest triumphs.

Salmon have an incredibly impressive sense of smell. Atlantic Salmon can smell one drop of scent within an area equivalent to ten Olympic swimming pools!

26

FORTH BRIDGE

'The Forth Bridge flings its three double steel cantilevers across the water to the Kingdom of Fife. It is the most familiar bridge in the world.

It is seen on posters, framed in railway carriages and in all kinds of books. To see the Forth Bridge is rather like meeting a popular actress, but with this difference: it exceeds expectations.

'It is a memorable sight. It is more impressive than its pictures. The proportions are so tremendous that you do not realise how vast they are until a train crosses over, skied above you in an intricate tracery of girders. Then you are astonished. It is even higher than it appeared without the train, and therefore longer and in every way more stupendous. The sound of trains crossing the Forth Bridge is a queer, fascinating and peculiar sound: something between a roar and a rumble, and with a hint of drums …'
– H. V. Morton, 1929

Since the first complete crossing of the bridge took place in February 1890, nothing has been built in Scotland that closely competes with the Forth Bridge for majesty or sheer scale. This is one of Scotland's very few Category A-listed buildings. One encyclopedia rightly describes it as 'the one immediately and internationally recognised Scottish landmark'.

In fact, its mass was no accident: the structure is actually overbuilt, with far more steel than was

needed, because – in the wake of the tragedy the other side of Fife – it was vital the Forth Bridge simply look strong and that the travelling public be reassured.

For it was not the first attempt at spanning the Queensferry narrows. Work had already begun on a suspension bridge here – the foundation stones already laid – to the design of an engineer named Thomas Bouch, when, on the night of 28 December 1879, in a high wind, the central span of the lattice-girder bridge he had thrown across the Firth of Tay collapsed.

With it, into the chill North Sea, went a six-carriage train and 75 lives. And Sir Thomas's reputation. The Forth and other projects were cancelled, bridges built to his designs were demolished, and he was – justly – damned at the subsequent inquiry. He lost his mind and was dead within the year.

The Tay Bridge Disaster appalled Britain and the world, and shook confidence in mighty engineering everywhere. So the new Forth Bridge had much to prove. The project now passed to a new double act, engineer John Fowler and designer Benjamin Baker, and the bridge was duly built by the men of Sir William Arrol & Co., Glasgow. The on-site engineer was Allan Stewart.

The new bridge was the first major structure in Britain to be built of steel (the Eiffel Tower, its contemporary, was constructed from wrought iron) and to a robust cantilever-style design: there are three mighty four-tower cantilevers, each on its own granite pier. In the light of the Tay tragedy, Baker also went to unprecedented lengths for the time in calculating, over and over again, anything that might bear on safety, for example the weight and frequency of traffic, the pressures of wind, the strain of changes in temperature, and 'erection stresses' – how components might be affected during the building works themselves.

The span of the Firth chosen, from Dalmeny in West Lothian to North Queensferry in Fife, was selected not just for brevity but also for its convenient natural features. The Forth Bridge makes use of Inchgarvie Island, the promontories on either shore, and the high banks above them, where empty space yawns beneath your railway carriage with delicious suddenness.

The Forth Bridge was completed in December 1889 and on 21 January 1890 there were determined test-loadings, using three weighty locomotives each hauling 50 coal-piled wagons. This was deliberately twice the bridge's design-load and, as they slowly processed, stopped and puffed slowly on again, engineers measured carefully for any deflection in the structure. It was well within the margin of safety. Only days earlier, the most violent winds ever recorded had howled in the Forth; brave experts upon the bridge found deflection of less than an inch.

In March 1890, the Forth Bridge was officially opened by the Prince of Wales (the future King Edward VII), who solemnly drove home the very last rivet.

In all, it had taken seven years to build, needed nearly 58,000 tonnes of metal (ten times as much as the Eiffel Tower), 6.5 million rivets and – even today – is studied the world over as a triumph of engineering, all the more so for its pioneering nature. It stands 330 feet tall, is 1.6 miles in length and supports a double railway track 150 feet above the Forth estuary at high tide. In total, it's been calculated that the entire superstructure weighs 51,324 tonnes, and, 114 years later, she still carries between 190 to 200 trains a day, providing a passenger link to Fife of such efficiency that all modern efforts to furnish a fast ferry crossing from Edinburgh to Kirkcaldy have foundered.

Passenger trains must observe a 50-mph speed limit; goods trains 20 mph. The standard weight limit for any train is 1,422 tonnes; this has been waived for the frequent coal trains, as long as only one train is crossing at a time. It should be remembered, of course, that modern locomotives are much lighter than their steaming Victorian forebears.

The construction was, of course, for the North British Railway, who contributed 35 per cent of the cost; the rest was raised from three English rail concerns who fed into the NBR's east coast Scottish services, and the Forth Bridge was jointly owned by them (and their two final successors) until the nationalisation of Britain's railways in 1947. The structure is now owned by Network Rail Infrastructure Ltd.

Scots still compare any tedious, never-ending commitment to 'painting the Forth Bridge', in the widespread belief that, so vast was the pile, painting was continuous, a new coat being applied as soon as weary men had finished the first. This was largely myth and, after a programme of thorough shot-blasting to the bare metal from 2002, a new and very tough paint (if in the same ruddy shade) was painstakingly applied. Completed in 2011, it's expected to last at least 25 years, and perhaps 40.

The Forth Bridge survived German bombing on 16 October 1939, and since 1990 (with a two-year hiatus during the recent repainting) she has been beautifully floodlit at night.

For all her fame and grace, we should not forget that the Forth Bridge cost rather more than cash and steel: at least 73 men were killed during her construction, hundreds more were crippled – and a log book of accidents and sickness during that time records some 26,000 incidents. A sobering thought below those high girders. In 2012, the First Minister Alex Salmond unveiled twin memorials, in North and South Queensferry, to the thousands of 'Briggers' who contributed to building, maintaining and restoring the structure since construction began.

27

IRN-BRU

Innocently described as a 'citrus flavoured soft drink', the iconic IRN-BRU really does have iron in it – any measure is 0.002 per cent ammonium ferric citrate.

Little more is known, save that there are 32 flavouring agents, including quinine and caffeine. In fact, for both brand protection and a certain dash of drama and mystique, there is only one written copy of the elixir's precise formula on the planet (kept in a Swiss bank vault).

Launched by Robert Barr and his son, Andrew Gregg Barr, in the foundry town of Falkirk in 1901, it was originally named 'Iron Brew' until 1946, when lawmakers proposed banning brand names that weren't 'literally true'. It thereby became IRN-BRU. In recent decades the brand has become both admired and notorious as a result of its original TV commercials.

Although he retired as chairman of A.G. Barr in 2009, Robin, great nephew of the original Robert Barr, still personally mixes the syrup – alone, with high security – at the company's headquarters in Cumbernauld. Only three people alive know the recipe by memory. Robin has shared the details with his daughter, Julie, currently A.G. Barr's lawyer, who will one day inherit the priestly rite, and the identity of the other is a closely guarded secret.

It's hard, in any event, to argue with an extraordinarily refreshing fizz – a big part of its appeal is that IRN-BRU is not too sweet – which, besides its cherished role as a national hangover cure, remains the top-selling soft drink in Scotland, the fifth-bestselling in the United Kingdom, and is also produced under licence in, for instance, Spain and Russia. There has been an additional plant recently opened in Milton Keynes and a factory in Moscow. It is also exported on a large scale, though the IRN-BRU you drink in Australia tastes slightly

*A late 1930s' example of
point-of-sale material used
for 'Iron Brew'.*

different, as her laws don't permit caffeine and quinine in clear soft drinks.

Scots do take rather a dark pleasure in a near-unique achievement: we're one of just two countries on the planet (the other being Peru, where Inka Kola holds sway) where the most popular soft drink is not Coca-Cola, to the abiding and gibbering frustration of its American executives. What's more, IRN-BRU is steadily capturing a bigger share of the English market every year, and might one day overhaul its stateside rival on both sides the border.

The sheer audacity of this doubtless underpins the cheek that has long marked Irn Bru advertising. For many years, they ran with the wry (and very Scottish) slogan, 'Your other national drink'. Then, in the 1980s, it was 'Made in Scotland. From girders', the TV spots showing a range of characters with super-strong or magnetic powers and, in a send-up of the 1980 wartime weepie 'Yanks', beginning what has proved to be a lucrative vein in parody. With the new slogan, 'It's fizzy, its ginger, it's phenomenal!', for instance, one costly but fantastically choreographed 2009 advert was a spoof of High School Musical and a 2006 animated mock of The Snowman ('He took my IRN-BRU and then let go of my hand!') is still, each December, regularly screened as an early sign of Christmas.

Other adverts have landed A.G. Barr in occasional trouble, from their portrayal of feisty criminal pensioners and the 1950s housewife who 'used to be a man' to IRN-BRU-related dramas in the delivery suite or the operating theatre. Oddly enough, the one that caused most frisson was a mere billboard poster of a cow, over the slogan, 'When I'm a burger, I want to be washed down with IRN-BRU'. There were more than 700 complaints, but it was cleared by advertising watchdogs.

Though theirs is a publicly floated company, the Barr family remain very much part of the business and there was widespread Scottish pleasure in 2013 when a proposed merger with the Britvic drinks empire fell through. The brand marches perkily on: some 980 people are employed at ten sites around the UK; Sir Sean Connery chose a crate of IRN-BRU for his personal celebrity exhibit at Edinburgh's Museum of Scotland ... and twenty cans of the fizz, we are assured, are sold every second.

An advertisement from the mid-1970s featuring 'Popeye' consuming a can of IRN-BRU to give him strength instead of his customary spinach.

An amusing, but suggestive, poster from 2001.

116

28

SIR SEAN CONNERY

Born in a tenement in Edinburgh, on
25 August 1930, Thomas Sean Connery
is probably the most famous Scot on the
planet. Long an international movie star,
he is still, for most, the definitive James Bond.

He is particularly cherished by his countrymen, as he has refused to shed his native tones – playing an Irish-American policeman and a Soviet submarine captain, never mind 007, in the same crisp, amused Scottish accent.

His dad, Joe, was a lorry driver; his mum, Euphemia McLean, kept house. Joe was poorly paid, and his taste for drink and gambling further depleted the family budget. They could not even afford a cradle and their firstborn spent his earliest months in a drawer. 'We were very poor,' says Sir Sean, 'but I never knew how poor because that's how everyone was there.'

Little Tommy lived largely on the streets, playing on the cobbled roads and constantly ripping his well-worn shorts. Though he had an aptitude for maths, he was not of an aspirational home and left school at 13 to work full time at St Cuthbert's Co-operative Dairy. (Then, and for many years thereafter, its milk was delivered around Edinburgh by

'Everything I've done has had to be accomplished in my own cycle, my own time, on my own behalf, and with my own sweat. But if people hadn't liked what I was doing, I'd probably be delivering milk today – and I never forget that.' Sean Connery.

horse-drawn floats.) Improbable numbers still claim to have had their daily pint delivered by 'Big Tam'.

Ill health ended a three-year stint in the Royal Navy, though it left Connery with two unimaginative tattoos – SCOTLAND FOREVER and 'Mum and Dad'. Dark, hard, handsome, he struggled through various grotty jobs: bricklaying, coal-shovelling, nude life-modelling at the city's Art School and even a stint polishing coffins.

His journey into acting began not with some revelation of high culture but a growing interest in bodybuilding. 'It was not so much to be fit but to look good for the girls,' he recalled cheerfully. However, gym-mates were sufficiently impressed in 1953 to nominate him for the Mr Universe contest. 'Mr Scotland', as he cheekily styled himself, came third in the Tall Men section – and caught the eye of a casting director looking for suitable male totty

for the chorus-line of a forthcoming Drury Lane production of *South Pacific*.

'I didn't have a voice, didn't dance,' Sir Sean would crack decades later, 'but I could look good standing there.' After the first rehearsal, he was addicted and shrewdly discarded his first name; the show's programme lists 'Sean Connery' for the first time. He won increasingly better roles in assorted films and television dramas, but, bothered by his lack of education – 'I didn't want people thinking of me as some lout' – he began reading widely: Proust, Tolstoy, Dostoevsky. Not that he has ever lost the feral instincts of mean streets …

And the accent, as we might in a more egalitarian age forget, had one huge advantage: it made Connery singularly classless, neither posh nor bourgeois nor common.

In 1957, Connery fell for Australian actress Diane Cilento and the couple wed. When in 1959 she fell ill with tuberculosis, he unhesitatingly passed up what would have been a huge break (a big part in *El Cid*, alongside Charlton Heston) to be with her. It was a noble choice that did him no harm: Twentieth Century Fox came calling with a contract.

In 1961, producers Harry Saltzman and Albert 'Cubby' Broccoli offered him the lead in a series of spy movies based on the new and best-selling novels of Ian Fleming. Connery was not immediately enthusiastic. Nor was Fleming, who thought the Scot 'unrefined'. Besides, Connery had been steadily balding since early manhood (and would wear a toupee in all the films). But Dana Broccoli saw something – sexiness, charisma, danger – and persuaded her husband the Scot was the right choice. Saltzman was convinced on sight. 'We all knew this guy had something. We signed him without a screen test. He was 007.'

Director Terence Young was entranced by Connery, and as Lois Maxwell, who played Miss Moneypenny, fondly remembered, 'Terence took Sean under his wing.' There followed a crash course in etiquette; Young taught Connery 'the ways of being dapper, witty, and above all cool'.

If doubts had lingered, the spectacular success of the first Bond film, *Dr. No* (premiered in London in October 1962), silenced them. The film grossed hundreds of thousands of pounds in just two weeks and would end up, globally, making nearly $60 million. President Kennedy even insisted on a private screening in the White House.

While Connery would make four Bond movies in rapid succession, he also found time for other roles, notably Alfred Hitchcock's *Marnie* (1964) and *The Hill* (1965). After George Lazenby's solitary outing in *On Her Majesty's Secret Service* (1969) – the Australian would not commit to a series – Connery agreed to reprise the role in *Diamonds Are Forever*, coolly demanding (and getting) the colossal fee of £1,250,000 – the equivalent of £23 million today – which he devoted to his own charity, the Scottish International Education Trust. In 1983, he made one final cheeky appearance as 007 in *Never Say Never Again*.

By 1974 he was spending most of the year in Marbella. He was by this stage a committed supporter of the Scottish National Party (his politics undoubtedly delayed his knighthood, bestowed only in 2000. Legislation by the Labour Government in 2001, prohibiting donations to any British political party by anyone living abroad, was almost certainly

Sean Connery is for many the definitive James Bond. He played 007 six time, in Dr. No (1962); From Russia With Love (1963), Goldfinger (1964) – thought by many to be the best; Thunderball (1965); You Only Live Twice (1967); Diamonds Are Forever (1971); and Never Say Never Again (1983).

to spite the SNP and Sir Sean, a singularly generous benefactor: 'I'm not shy about voicing what I believe to be true …')

By the early 1970s, Connery was well into his forties and increasingly landed character parts or cameos. Notable parts include *Robin and Marian* (1976), the over-edited but still haunting *The Name of the Rose* (1986), *Indiana Jones and the Last Crusade* (1989), *The Hunt for Red October* (1990), *The Rock* (1996) and *The League of Extraordinary Gentleman* (2003). He was unforgettable in 1987's *The Untouchables*, for which he collected an Oscar for Best Supporting Actor.

DID YOU KNOW?

Connery's first job was in Edinburgh was as a milkman at the St. Cuthberts Co-operative Society. Following this he joined the Royal Navy.

Connery came third in 1950's Mr. Universe competition.

James Bond author, Ian Fleming, initially opposed the selection of Connery as Bond. It was producer Cubby Broccoli's wife, Dana Broccoli, who championed Connery, believing he would make the perfect 007.

During the filming of *Thunderball* Connery very nearly lost his life when a shark broke through the separation between the two tanks they were swimming in. Luckily, he managed to abandon the water immediately.

29

THE EDINBURGH FESTIVAL

Every August, and for three weeks, Scotland's capital
– one of the most beautiful cities in the world – is
dominated by an extravaganza of the performing arts.

Visitors descend by the tens of thousands, there is soon not a room to be had, the desperate think nothing of renting entire houses for the duration, the city's population is whispered to double and Edinburgh's six main theatres and concert-halls – to say nothing of some lesser or unconventional venues – boast some of the finest actors, musicians and ensembles through the twilight of a northern summer.

And the original Edinburgh International Festival has pupped other parallel delights – notably the Edinburgh Festival Fringe, by far the bigger event, much more loosely organised and with thousands of acts from the acclaimed to the quietly insane in assorted church halls or marquees on the Meadows;

the Edinburgh Book Festival – launched in 1983 – the Edinburgh Film Festival, the Edinburgh Television Festival (frightfully precious and invitation-only) and, perhaps most famously, the Military Tattoo on the Esplanade of Edinburgh Castle, whose pipes first skirled in August 1950, once the Army eagerly muscled in on the act.

It was all born as the dust settled after the Second World War, and by the vision of Rudolf Bing, an Austrian-born opera impresario of well-to-do Jewish parents who had prudently settled themselves in Britain

after Hitler came to power in Germany. After all that followed, and as peace descended upon a Europe in rubble, Bing became determined to launch an annual arts festival somewhere in the United Kingdom, and Henry Harvey Wood of the British Council pondered the location hard:

Certain preconditions were obviously required of such a centre. It should be a town of reasonable size, capable of absorbing and entertaining anything between 50,000 and 150,000 visitors over a period of three weeks to a month. It should, like Salzburg, have considerable scenic and picturesque appeal and it should be set in a country likely to be attractive to tourists and foreign visitors. It should have sufficient number of theatres, concert halls and open spaces for the adequate staging of a programme of an ambitious and varied character. Above all it should be a city likely to embrace the opportunity and willing to make the festival a major preoccupation not only in the City Chambers but in the heart and home of every citizen, however modest. Greatly daring but not without confidence I recommended Edinburgh as the centre and promised to make preliminary investigations.

That Edinburgh had suffered scarcely a bomb during the war and was readily reached by road and rail were other selling-points – and the enthusiastic support of the city's Lord Provost, Sir John Falconer, settled the question.

Late in 1945, a committee was set up, which soon determined that the earliest practicable date to begin the first Edinburgh International Festival would be 24 August 1947, and to 'provide a platform for the flowering of the human spirit'. The inaugural programme was dominated by classical music and the

Promoted as the world's greated platform for creative freedom the Edinburgh Festival Fringe allows 'open access', which means anyone may particpate with any type of performance – and so the almost month-long event is amazingly democratic and diverse.

most memorable, moving experience was the reunion, after those recent and terrible years, of conductor Bruno Walter with the Vienna Philharmonic Orchestra. 'What you have done in Edinburgh is one of the most magnificent experiences since the war,' the joyous Walter declared. 'Here human relations have been renewed.'

But eight companies of actors also turned up in the city, uninvited, found premises for themselves – quite independently of each other and with no overseeing organisation – and put on shows at the same time. It would be a year or two before someone coined the name, but thus the Festival Fringe (which is now lightly but centrally overseen) was launched. And the official Festival's first great dramatic success was the staging, in 1948 and in the Church of Scotland's General Assembly Hall, of Sir David Lindsay's *Ane Satyre of The Thrie Estaitis* – to huge acclaim, and its first performance since 1552.

The decades since have not been without their challenges. One can never be quite sure of the weather this far north. 'For Edinburgh in August,' joked journalist and critic Bernard Levin, 'dress as for Reykjavik in February.' For many years a mean minority in Edinburgh local government openly resented the event and any related public expenditure – it was 1994, with the dramatic reconstruction of what now became the Festival Theatre, before there was a genuine opera-house.

As for the Edinburgh Festival Fringe, it is now the largest arts-event in the world (typically, 3,000 shows on each August), and the very streets of the Old Town now ring with performers of all sorts of things as you struggle down the cobbles of the Royal Mile

– fire-eaters, jugglers, radical takes on Shakespeare, Brexit as pondered in interpretative dance… much of it simply, joyously nuts.

But the true star is this capital, those medieval thoroughfares, that glorious skyline, the changeful northern skies. 'This is a city of shifting light, of changing skies, of sudden vistas,' once mused Edinburgh author Alexander McCall Smith, 'A city so beautiful it breaks the heart again and again.'

30

SIR ANDY MURRAY

Andrew Barron Murray, born in Dunblane, Perthshire, in May 1987, is the greatest British male tennis player since the 1930s.

In August 2012 he blew away Roger Federer to win the Gold Medal at the London Olympics, and the following month defeated Novak Djokovic in a 5-set thriller to win the US Open – and, on 7 July 2013, once more against Djokovic in baking conditions and in straight sets, became the first British man to win Wimbledon since Fred Perry in 1936. These achievements alone have sealed his greatness, securing him an OBE and, in December 2013 and by public vote, BBC Sports Personality of the Year.

Yet Murray – tall, gawky, of flat conversational style and extraordinary if focused aggression on court – remains very, very Scottish; and it has not made life easy for him. In Britain, tennis is a sport predominantly of English middle-class privilege and largely managed by the languid Lawn Tennis Association, to whom Murray owes nothing. Though his genius on court was early apparent, it was burnished from his early teens by the kindness of sponsors and the sacrifice of his parents, and he first really came to public attention at Wimbledon in 2005, when the wild-carded 18-year old reached the third round and eclipsed England's favourite, Tim Henman. The Scot besides made an imprudent online joke in 2006 when, asked whom he favoured for the World Cup, cracked 'Anyone but England!' It was not particularly funny, but nor was it particularly offensive – yet it extracted extraordinary odium.

It's been a long and winding road for the boy from Dunblane, who as an eight-year old in March 1996 survived the appalling massacre at the town's primary school, being sheltered in the headmaster's study as crazed loner Thomas Hamilton gunned down sixteen defenceless children, their teacher and, finally, himself. (Andy Murray still cannot discuss that day without weeping.) He has been beset through his career by injury, forced to sit out Wimbledon in 2007 on account of a dodgy knee – the bones in one patella have never fused – and starting uncertainly in 2014 after a back operation. But his greatest frustration has been his era. A player of Murray's extraordinary touch and power would, in the 1990s, have swept all before him. In the twenty-first century, he has had to contend instead with the greatest players the sport has ever produced – Roger Federer, Rafael Nadal, Novak Djokovic – and his triumphs are all the more impressive for that.

Andy Murray's wedding to his long-term girlfriend Kim Sears in a ceremony in his hometown of Dumblane in April 2015.

For years it seemed his greatest opponent was himself – given on occasion to snatching defeat from the jaws of victory, berating himself after some error and then losing several games in succession. His first serve has never been entirely reliable (though, when on song, it thwacks like an Exocet), and the true strengths of his game are excellent return of service and perhaps the best backhand in the business, capable of extraordinary feats from preposterous positions and under the most fantastic pressure. Under the tutelage of Ivan Lendl, though – his coach from 2012 to 2014 – a new unflappability became apparent, and Murray besides has been steadied by contented domesticity with the serene, pretty Kim Sears, their daughters and their scruffy Border terriers

He's essentially a 'counter-puncher,' commentator Dan Thorp has noted astutely, favouring long rallies from the baseline and soaking an opponent's energy before, in a flash, changing from defensive to offensive and with low fast ground-strokes to the lines of lethal accuracy. According to Henman, Murray has 'the best lob in the business' and, throughout his career, the Scot has had a fondness for the cheeky and infuriating drop-shot – though it doesn't always pay off. Indeed, such is the racking drama of a typical Andy Murray match – highs and lows, agonies and ecstasies, aching tension and uncertainty of outcome – that you rather want to watch from behind the sofa.

When training, Murrary would have extraoridinary discipline – rigorous coaching, exercise, weight-training, stretches, Bikram yoga, long and gasping ice-baths. He would also follow a rigorous diet, consuming 6,000 calories a day washed down with six litres of plain water – six meals daily, launched with a breakfast of yoghurt,

a peanut butter bagel and a protein-shake. Red meat and pasta are prominent but in particular he is said to devour a great deal of fish. 'Team Murray' is charged to find a high-end sushi restaurant wherever he happens to be playing, and he always has a large meal within an hour of finishing a match. Alcohol, processed food and sugar are of course wholly eschewed.

After losing his first Wimbledon final – to Roger Federer, in July 2012 – the Scot conceded with such grace and cried so unabashedly as to soften many English hearts. In a BBC TV profile in 2013, besides, the public saw many new aspects of him, from the happy and banter-dotted hours of coaching and therapy with 'Team Murray' to the genuine affection, off-court, between Murray, Nadal and Djokovic. He may have career prize-earnings north of $30 million – to say nothing of what he makes in advertising and endorsement – and remain gruff, sardonic and shaggy; but the first Brit to win Wimbledon in short trousers is also an extraordinarily nice one.

In April 2014 Murray was honoured with the Freedom of Stirling; in 2015 he led the British tennis team to its first Davis Cup victory; and in 2016 won not only his second Wimbledon title but his second Olympic gold-medal, ending that year atop the APTP rankings as the No. 1 player in the world. Knighted the following year – Britain's youngest knight in modern times – in January 2019, tormented by a chronic hip problem, Sir Andy announced his coming retirement.

DID YOU KNOW?

In March 2005, at just 17 years old, Murray became the youngest Britain to play a Davis Cup match.

Andy's brother, Jamie, is also an extremely successful tennis player. He is a six-time Grand Slam doubles winner, a Davis Cup champion and a former doubles world No. 1 champion.

Murray supports many charities across the world and is the founding member of 'Malaria No More UK Leadership Council'.

In January 2019, Murray announced he would sadly be retiring that year from tennis due to a severe hip injury.

In recognition of his service to tennis, Murray was awarded the 'Freedom of Stirling' award and an honorary Doctorate from the University of Stirling.

Images reproduced courtesy of

01 Callanish Stones
8–9 Anneka/Shutterstock.com
10 Mark Heighes/Shutterstock.com

02 Whisky
12 Rebecca Schochenmaier/
Shutterstock.com
14 Rebecca Schochenmaier/
Shutterstock.com
15 ZRyzner/Shutterstock.com

03 Honours of Scotland
16–17 © Crown Copyright HES.
Licensor Scran.ac.uk
19 Anton_Ivanov/Shutterstock.com

04 Eilean Donan
20–1 Mikadun/Shutterstock.com
22–3 TTPhoto/Shutterstock.com

05 Gaelic
24–5 Natasa Kirin/Shutterstock.com
26 Sorley MacLean © Cailean
MacLean
26 Alasdair Scott, Bun-sgoil Taobh
na Pairce An Comunn
27 David Madison/Getty Images

06 Bagpipes
28–9 Lukassek/Shutterstock.com
30 (funeral procession) Emory
Kristof/National Geographic
Collection/Getty Images
30 (bagpipes) Nail Bikbaev/
Shutterstock.com
31 Maurice McDonald/PA Archive/
© PA Images

07 Golden Eagle
32–3 Glass and Nature/
Shutterstock.com
34 (eagle) Neil McIntyre
34 The Gleneagles Hotel
35 Nadezda Murmakova/
Shutterstock.com

08 Mary Queen of Scots
36 Traveler1116/Istock
38 HeartlandArts/Shutterstock.com
39 TreasureGalore/Shutterstock.com

09 Edinburgh Castle
40–1 Stockcube/Shutterstock.com
43 domhnall dods/Shutterstock.com

10 John Knox
44–5 Heartland Arts/
Shutterstock.com
46 Brendan Howard/
Shutterstock.com
47 Victor FlowerFly/
Shutterstock.com

11 Ben Nevis
48–9 Targn Pleiades/
Shutterstock.com
50 josefkubes/Shutterstock.com
51 Astudio/Shutterstock.com

12 Tartan
52–3 Paolo Gallo/Shutterstock.com
54 Jillain Cain Photography/
Shutterstock.com
55 Byunau Konstantin/
Shuttertock.com

13 Red Deer
56–7 Gail Johnson/
Shutterstock.com
58 Monarch of the Glen © National
Museums Scotland reproduced
by kind permission of Diageo
59 Mark Caunt/Shutterstock.com

14 Haggis
60–1 Paul Brighton/
Shutterstock.com
62 Monkey Business Images/
Shutterstock.com
63 StockCreations/
Shutterstock.com

15 Tweed
64–5 Sarah CC/Stockimo/
Alamy Stock Photo
66 EQRoy/Shutterstock.com
67 EQRoy/Shutterstock.com

16 Loch Lomond
68–9 Antony McAulay/
Shutterstock.com
70 Martin Fowler/Shutterstock.com

17 Highland Cattle
72–3 Shalith/Shutterstock.com
74 magnetix/Shutterstock.com

18 Robert Burns
76–7 Georgios Kollidas/
Shutterstock.com
78 Tristan Tan/Shutterstock.com
79 Everett Historical/
Shutterstock.com

19 Loch Ness
80–1 Botond Horvath/
Shutterstock.com
82 Bloomberg/Getty Images

20 PS Waverley
84–5 David Falconer/
Shutterstock.com
86 © Scottish Motor Museum Trust.
Licensor Scran.ac.uk
87 Cairns Aitken Licensor
Scran.ac.uk

22 Golf
92–3 Julietphotography/
Shutterstock.com
94 CE Photography/
Shutterstock.com
95 Jospeh Sohm/Shutterstock.com

23 Police
96–7 Tana88/Shutterstock.com
98 The Glasgow Police Museum
99 Tana888/Shutterstock.com

24 Robert Louis Stevenson
100–1 © National Portrait Gallery,
London
102 Leonard Zhukovsky/
Shutterstock.com

25 Salmon
104–5 Mark Caunt/Shutterstock.com
106 JASPERIMAGE/
Shutterstock.com
107 Mark Caunt/Shutterstock.com

26 Forth Bridge
108–9 Serge Bertasius Photography/
Shutterstock.com
110 NAS BR/FOR/4/34/138 (detail)
National Archive of Scotland
photographs by permission of
BRB (Residuary) Ltd
111 Loop Images Ltd/Alamy Stock
Photo

27 IRN-BRU
114–15 Images courtesy of
A. G Barr plc

28 Sir Sean Connery
116–17 Ullstein bild/Getty Images
(detail)
118 Jeff Kravitz/Getty Images
119 Ullstein bild/Getty Images

29 Edinburgh Festival
120–1 Moomusician/
Shutterstock.com
122 (top) Stephen Finn/
Shutterstock.com
(bottom) Skully/
Shutterstock.com
123 Lee Walker/Shutterstock.com

30 Sir Andy Murray
124–5 © PA
126 © PA